MICROSOFT PROJECT
in easy steps

John Carroll

COMPUTER STEP

In easy steps is an imprint of Computer Step
Southfield Road . Southam
Warwickshire CV33 OFB . England

Tel: 01926 817999 Fax: 01926 817005
http://www.computerstep.com

Notice of Liability
Every effort has been made to ensure that this book contains accurate
and current information. However, Computer Step and the author shall
not be liable for any loss or damage suffered by readers as a result of
any information contained herein.

Trademarks
Microsoft® and Windows® are registered trademarks of Microsoft
Corporation. All other trademarks are acknowledged as belonging to
their respective companies.

Printed and bound in the United Kingdom

ISBN 1-84078-015-0

Contents

14   Hyperlinks and HTML   149

15   PERT Charts   155

16   Programme Management   165

17   Advanced Topics   171

18   Project Methodology   179

Index   187

The Basics

This chapter explains what Microsoft Project is and how it can help you to manage your project. It provides some background to project management and then introduces the main features of Microsoft Project.

Chapter One

Covers

Introduction

Microsoft Project is a great project management tool. Managing projects can be a complex activity but, with the help of Microsoft Project, you can plan, schedule and control the progress of your project.

Why do you need to plan and control your project? Well, statistically, around 50% of business projects fail. If you don't plan and control your project, the chances are that it will be among that 50%!

REMEMBER

This book covers Microsoft Project 98 – some of the features may not be available in your version, but the essential features remain similar.

Whether your project is a simple short-term one (such as arranging a company meeting) or a more complex project (like developing a new computer system), Microsoft Project will let you stay in control.

Used as a planning tool, Microsoft Project can produce some great looking charts to help you plan your project.

But Project can do a lot more besides:

- It can help you allocate and schedule work, tasks and activities.

- It can produce a critical path analysis to identify where you will need to track progress carefully.

- It can identify if you have too much work allocated to any one person.

- It can schedule facilities such as meeting rooms and overhead projectors for you.

- It can interface with your e-mail system or Internet browser to allow you to keep your team in the picture.

- It can publish to the Web using HTML and export files to Excel so you can produce charts and graphs of your project's progress.

In short, while Project won't actually manage the project for you it will certainly help you manage it better.

How to use this Book

If you're new to Project Management
Start at the beginning and work right the way through to Chapter 11. Use our example project to build up experience and test things and try them out. Then go back to Chapter 2 and start again with your real project.

If you're new to Microsoft Project (but not to project management)
If you've used another project planning tool, then skim through Chapter 1 and start at Chapter 2 (the examples should illustrate any differences). If you've not used another project planning tool, then work through from Chapter 1 (but skim the topics on project management).

If you've used a previous version of Microsoft Project
Skim Chapters 1 and 2 then work through from Chapter 3 looking out for new features such as:

- Hyperlinks and HTML Publishing.

- Workgroup features.

- Resource contouring, levelling and task splitting.

- Resource Usage and Task Usage Views.

- New terminology (Fixed Unit Tasks) and defaults.

- Multiple resource rates and variable resource rates.

The exercises
The exercises through this book build up a project plan step-by-step.

Later topics build on the project and assume that you have saved it at the end of the previous topic.

If you have skipped any topics or chapters, don't worry, you should be able to see from the screen shots what's happening and be able to recreate them.

Installing Microsoft Project

 Although 30MB free space is the requirement for the typical installation, you will need more space if you wish to install some of the options under the custom installation. Try to start with 100MB or more of free space. The Setup program will warn you if you do not have enough room.

Installing Microsoft Project is done by running the program SETUP.EXE. If you have a CD-ROM version, this usually runs automatically when the CD is inserted into the drive.

Before running SETUP, make sure you have a suitable system. You need the following:

- A 486 (or higher specification) PC running Windows 95/98 or NT.

- At least 12MB of RAM (memory) on Windows 95/98 or 16MB on Windows NT.

- At least 30MB of free disk space.

- A CD-ROM drive (recommended). If you don't have a CD-ROM drive you can order a set of 3.5" disks from Microsoft.

 When installing large programs, it is easy to use almost all the space on your hard disk. Unfortunately, Windows needs free space for temporary files. You also need to allow for your documents. It is best to keep 50MB or more free at all times.

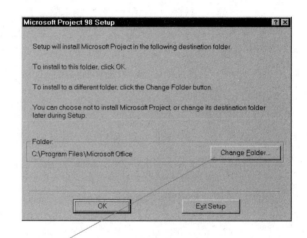

Click here to change the folder where Microsoft Project will be installed. Usually the only reason to change this setting is if you have another drive which has more free space available.

Next, the Setup program asks you to choose what type of installation you want. If you wish to have control over which elements of Microsoft Project are installed, choose Custom. Otherwise choose Typical for a standard installation.

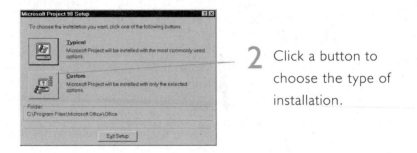

2 Click a button to choose the type of installation.

- Choose Typical to let the Setup programme decide which components to install. This is a good choice if you are new to Microsoft Project.

- Choose Custom if you want to choose exactly which components are installed. If you choose this option a further dialog lets you check the required options.

Finally you will be asked to select your combination of paper format (A4 or US letter) and dictionary (US, British or Australian English).

3 Click in the list to select the paper format and dictionary you want installed.

4 Click OK to complete the installation.

What is a Project?

A project is a controlled process designed to achieve an identified objective. The objective could be a personal one such as organising a foreign trip, a construction project like building a house, or a business project like implementing a new accounting system.

Whatever sort of project you have, there are three key characteristics that you can associate with it:

1. It must have an end result or outcome. There would be no point in carrying out a project if it did not achieve anything. Further, the end result must be wanted or have some sort of benefit; if not, there would be no point doing it.

2. It has to have a beginning or be initiated. Projects do not happen spontaneously, they need to be kicked off. But this step must come after the end result has been defined. If you were to initiate a project without knowing what you wanted to achieve, you would be likely to go round in ever decreasing circles!

3. It has to be carried out – the middle bit, getting from A to B. Again, things do not happen automatically just because you have defined your end result and initiated a project. The hard work comes in getting the project *successfully* from A to B.

Whatever your project is, Microsoft Project can help you reach your objective successfully.

Project Management

Projects need to be managed if they are going to be successful. So, is project management the same thing as ordinary management?

Ordinary management is involved with managing a process. It could be a department issuing invoices. It could be a factory producing widgets. It could be a telephone call centre. Whatever it is, managing it is a continuous process. Unless they go out of business, the department will continue issuing invoices, the factory will continue producing widgets and the call centre will continue dealing with calls.

On the other hand, a project begins when it is initiated and ends when it has achieved its goal. It has a finite life. Project management is the management of change.

The Project Manager's role is to steer the project successfully from its beginning to its end and deal with anything that happens along the way.

The Gantt Chart

The first thing you see when you open or create a new project is the Gantt chart.

It is the default view, and with good reason. The Gantt chart is probably the most useful project management tool.

They say that every picture tells a thousand words – this is the key picture in your project.

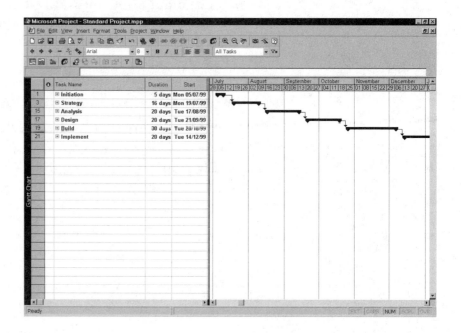

At the summary level you can view the whole project on one screen or on one sheet of paper. The Gantt chart represents the most frequently used way of representing a project.

The Gantt chart view is more than just a view, though. It also allows you to plan and control your project by inserting and editing project tasks, setting and changing project milestones and even allocating and controlling project resources.

Tasks and Milestones

At the detailed level in Gantt chart view, you can view the individual Tasks and Project Milestones.

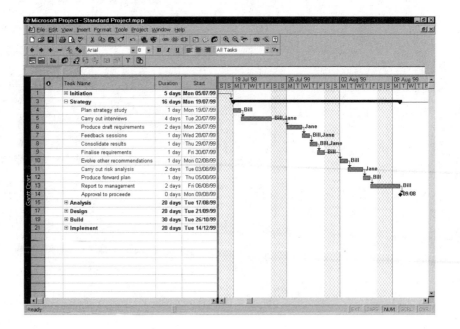

In Gantt Chart view you can:

- Expand or close up the list of tasks by clicking on the "+" or "-" beside any summary task.

- See and edit the scheduled start date, duration and finish date for each task.

- See and edit the linkages and dependencies between tasks.

- Set and change your project milestones.

- See who is allocated to each task and, if necessary, change the allocation.

Resource Usage

Resources are the people and facilities that you will use on your project. You can track resource usage through both the Task Usage and Resource Usage views.

The Task Usage view allows you to see who and what is being used on each Task:

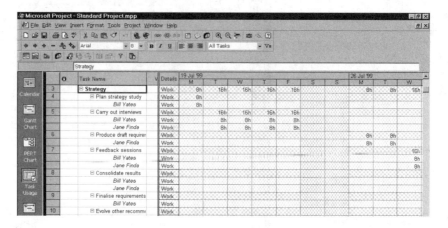

While the Resource Usage view allows you to see what each person is doing:

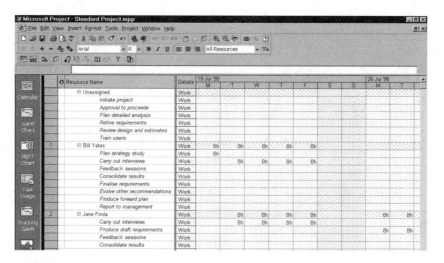

This enables you to monitor work assignments, identify potential problems through overload and generally stay in firm control of your project.

View Bar

While the Gantt Chart view is the default (and probably the most useful) view in Microsoft Project, there are another 25 pre-defined views. These are selected through the View Bar.

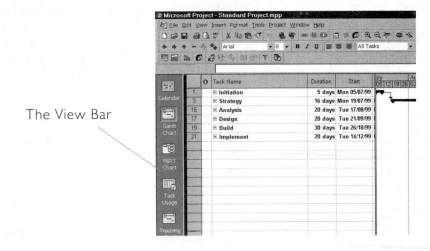

The View Bar

The View Bar can be used to switch back and forth between views. These are the views and their icons:

	Calendar	a monthly calendar showing tasks and their duration.
	Gantt Chart	the default view of tasks and time.
	PERT Chart	a network chart of tasks and their dependencies.
	Task Usage	tasks and who is allocated to them.
	Tracking Gantt	shows actuals against scheduled.
	Resource Graph	shows usage or cost of a resource over time.
	Resource Sheet	shows details of each resource.
	Resource Usage	shows a list of task assignments by resource.
	More Views	gives a list of all available views.

Toolbar

The Standard and Formatting Toolbars contain the usual Windows buttons and a number of Microsoft Project specific ones.

The buttons are:

 You can always find out what any button does by pausing the mouse pointer over it.

New Project

Open

Save

Print

Print preview

Spell Check

Cut

Copy

Paste

Format painter

Undo

Insert hyperlink

Web toolbar

Link Tasks

Unlink Tasks

Split Task

Resource information

Notes

Assign Resources

Zoom In

Zoom out

Go to selected task

Chart snapshot

Chart wizard

Help

Formatting

Outdent

Indent

Show Subtasks

Hide Subtasks

Hide assignments

Show all subtasks

Autofilter

How to get Help

There are several ways of getting help in Microsoft Project.

From the Menu Bar:

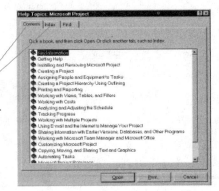

1 Select Help > Contents and Index.

2 Select the Contents Tab for a full list of contents, or the Index Tab for a searchable Index.

Use the F1 Key or click Help on the Button bar to open the Office Assistant.

HANDY TIP

If you want to know what something is, use Shift+F1 then point and click at the item you want to know about.

1 Type in your question.

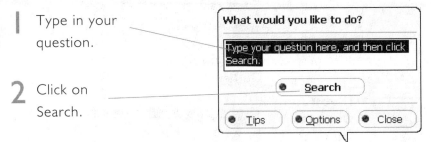

2 Click on Search.

You can even get Help from the Web using Help > Microsoft on the Web from the Menu Bar:

1 Make sure you have a Web connection.

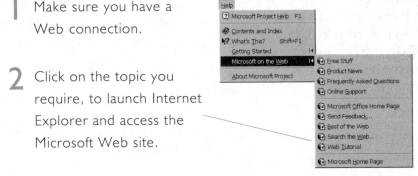

2 Click on the topic you require, to launch Internet Explorer and access the Microsoft Web site.

Quick Preview

For a bit more information about the concepts of project management and an overview of the capabilities of Project, you can take a quick preview.

The first time you start Microsoft Project, the Welcome dialog box appears. Click 'Watch A Quick Preview'.

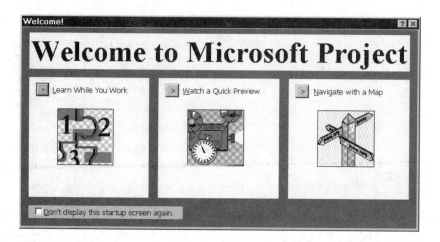

If the Welcome dialog box does not open, click Help > Getting Started > Quick Preview on the Menu Bar.

If you want to skip the Quick Preview for now, move on to Managing your project. You can always go back and have a look at the Quick Preview later.

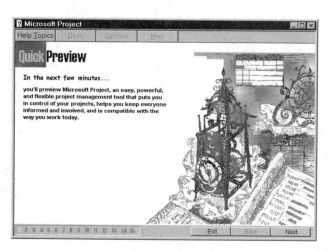

Follow the on-screen instructions for an overview of the capabilities of Project and how you can use it to plan your project.

Managing Your Project

This chapter introduces a structured approach to managing a project and explores the ways in which Microsoft Project can help you manage your project.

Chapter Two

A 4-Step Approach

Project management is the management of change.

In order to manage change and therefore manage your project, you need to carry out a number of steps or tasks.

In 'What is a project?' we defined a project as having a beginning, a middle and an end. If we expand the middle bit (carrying it out) into two steps we will have a 4-step approach to project management:

Experienced project managers may feel this is a simplistic approach. It is, but be patient as we will build on it in later sections.

1 Identify what you are trying to achieve – define your objectives.

2 Plan how you will get there – map out what you are going to do.

3 Carry it out – do it or manage it.

4 Hand it over – once the project is completed you have finished your job.

Interestingly, the difficult step for some project managers is the last one. They find it difficult to let go.

The project manager's job is to implement change. Once that change has been implemented their role as a project manager is completed. The new, changed state becomes a production process and that requires production (rather than project) management.

In the remainder of this section we will expand on each of these four steps and look at what is involved.

Step 1 – Define Your Objectives

The first step in any project is to define your objectives.

You need to define your objectives in order to be able to:

• Make sure you have identified the right target.

• Focus the other members of the project team on what the project is about.

• Create team commitment to and agreement about the project objectives.

• Ensure that you involve all interested parties in achieving a successful project outcome.

When you set out to define your objectives remember the acronym **SMART**. Objectives need to be: **S**pecific; **M**easurable; **A**greed; **R**ealistic; and **T**imed.

Specific
if your objectives are too vague they will be misunderstood. They should say exactly what the project is to achieve. A '10% reduction in stock' is much more specific than 'lower stock levels'. A 'two-day order turn-round time' is much more specific than 'faster order processing'.

Measurable
if you can't measure your achievements how will you know if you've achieved any?

Agreed
if the rest of the business and the rest of the project team have not agreed with the objectives, there will be no commitment to these objectives.

Realistic
if the objectives are not realistic, the project team will soon realise that and lose any commitment to the project.

Timed
if there is no pressure to complete the project it will never get completed.

REMEMBER

When you define your objectives, make sure that they are SMART.

So think about your project objectives now. Have you defined them adequately and are they SMART?

Keep it Simple

Another useful acronym to remember when thinking about your project objectives is KISS. It stands for: Keep It Simple, Stupid!

Your objectives should not only be SMART, they also need to be simple to understand. If not someone out there will misunderstand them!

If you don't keep it simple, this is a little reminder of what can go wrong:

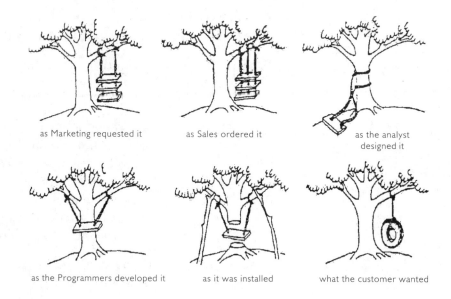

as Marketing requested it   as Sales ordered it   as the analyst designed it

as the Programmers developed it   as it was installed   what the customer wanted

REMEMBER

KISS: Keep It Simple (or you will be) Stupid.

So spend some more time making sure that your project objectives are stated simply. Make sure you know what you want to achieve then make sure other people do. The best way of doing that is to show your objectives to other people and ask them for their feedback.

Starting a Project

Start Microsoft Project by clicking on Start > Programs > Microsoft Project. Microsoft Project opens in Gantt Chart view with a blank project file and you can begin entering information about your project.

1 Click Project > Project Information on the Menu Bar. The Project Information dialog box opens.

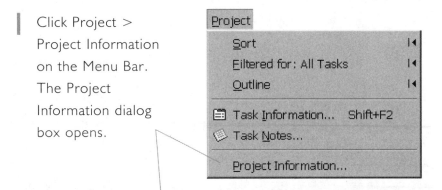

HANDY TIP **The default is for the project to be scheduled forward from the start date. You can also backward schedule by selecting 'Schedule from: Project Finish Date'.**

2 By default, the Start date will be the current date. If you want to change it click the control beside the date box to open a calendar and select the date.

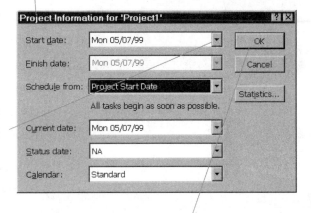

3 When you're happy with your start date, click the OK button.

Entering Summary Information

Once you've opened your project and set the start date you should enter your objectives and other summary information.

1 Click File > Properties on the Menu Bar and the Project Properties dialog box opens at the Summary tab.

2 Type the Title, Subject, your name and your Company name (if relevant).

3 Enter the type of project and any Keywords that could help you or someone else find the file in future.

Project1 Properties

General | Summary | Statistics | Contents | Custom

Title: Strategy Study

Subject: Financial Review

Author: Your Name

Manager: Your Name

Company: Your Company Plc

Category: Strategic Review

Keywords: strategy, finance, review

Comments: To carry out a 6 week study in order to determine if there is a business requirement for a new financial accounting system.

Hyperlink base:

Template:

☐ Save preview picture

OK   Cancel

4 Now type your project objectives into the Comments field.

5 Click OK. You have now started your project and entered your summary information.

Now you can move onto 'Step 2 – Developing Your Plan'.

Step 2 – Developing Your Plan

Once you've defined your project objectives, the next step is to plan how you will achieve them, how you will get there.

Before we start building the plan we need to look at some of the key things that make up a project plan. These are:

- Tasks

- Deliverables

- Milestones

- Resources

Tasks

Tasks are the basic building blocks of the project. In order to carry out a project you need to carry out a sequence of tasks.

Deliverables

HANDY TIP

Deliverables not only allow you to measure completion; they also allow you to carry out quality assurance.

Deliverables (sometimes referred to as Products) are the things that the project will produce along the way. Typically reports, requirements documents and acceptance certificates.

Milestones

Milestones are the points during the project when you can accurately measure your progress. They will typically be major events like approval to proceed or final acceptance.

Resources

Resources are the people and other things you will use on the project to carry out the tasks and produce the deliverables.

Your project plan will consist of the tasks needed to produce the deliverables and complete the project together with the resources you will use to perform them and the milestones you will use to measure your progress.

We will now look at these in a bit more detail.

Key Tasks and Deliverables

Any project consists of a number of tasks which need to be completed. It may consist of very few tasks or a very large number. Some tasks will be short tasks and others will take longer to complete. Some will be critical to the success of the project, while others may be less important.

The first step in producing your project plan is to begin listing the key tasks – the important ones, the ones that are critical to the success of the project. These will typically be related to a key deliverable. For example, if you were building a house, there would be a 'design' task which would have the 'house plans' as its deliverable.

If your project was to carry out a strategy study, the key tasks and deliverables would be something like:

Don't start typing in these tasks yet. We will do that in Chapter 3.

Key Tasks	Deliverables
Plan the study	Project Plan
Information gathering	Interview Notes
Produce draft requirements	Draft Requirements
Hold feedback sessions	Final Requirements
Develop recommendations	Recommendations
Perform risk analysis	Risk Analysis
Produce implementation plan	Implementation Plan
Report to management	Final Report

While you may well have many other tasks to carry out during your project and may have other deliverables you need to produce, these should represent the major ones.

If you are not sure about whether a task is a key task or not, then play safe and include it. It is easy enough to remove something later if it's not required but missing something important could cause major problems later.

Project Milestones

Project Milestones are the events that mark the completion of a major task or group of tasks in a project.

Typical Milestones would be the decision to proceed, selection of a supplier, acceptance of a major piece of work and of course completion of the project. Milestones often mark the acceptance of a key deliverable.

HANDY TIP

Although a milestone will usually have zero duration, it is possible to set a milestone that is also a task.

A Milestone normally has a zero duration. In other words, it marks a single point in time when something happens.

Once you have identified the key tasks and their deliverables in your project, you need to identify the major milestones. For a short project (such as our strategy study) there may be only one milestone – completion of the project.

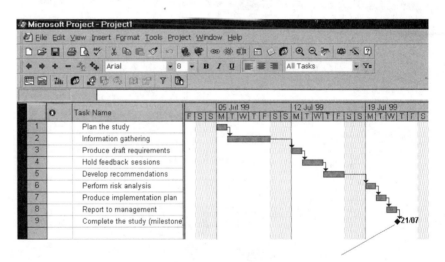

Project Milestone

For a longer project there will be more. Typically somewhere between three and eight.

Now look back at your key tasks and identify what your project milestones should be.

Resources

The key resources on most projects are people: the project manager (you) and anyone else you are going to use to do any work on the project.

| Click on Resource Sheet in the View Bar. The Resource Sheet view opens.

 HANDY TIP

You can also open resource sheet by clicking View > Resource Sheet on the Menu Bar.

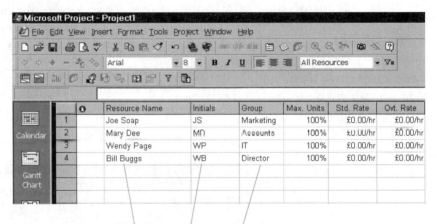

2 Type in the names, initials and group for all the people who will be involved on your project.

3 Then identify any other resources or facilities that your project will need and type them in after the people.

	❶	Resource Name	Initials	Group	Max. Units	Std. Rate	Ovt. Rate
1		Joe Soap	JS	Marketing	100%	£0.00/hr	£0.00/hr
2		Mary Dee	MD	Accounts	100%	£0.00/hr	£0.00/hr
3		Wendy Page	WP	IT	100%	£0.00/hr	£0.00/hr
4		Bill Buggs	WB	Director	100%	£0.00/hr	£0.00/hr
5		Project Room	P	Facilities	100%	£0.00/hr	£0.00/hr
6		Personal Computer	PC	Facilities	100%	£0.00/hr	£0.00/hr
7		Board Room	B	Facilities	100%	£0.00/hr	£0.00/hr
8		Overhead Projector	O	Facilities	100%	£0.00/hr	£0.00/hr

Don't worry about the other columns in the Resource Sheet; we will be dealing with them later.

The Full Monty

While the Gantt Chart presents a good visual representation of the project plan – you may need to produce a more formal project planning document at the end of the planning exercise. This will be particularly likely if it is a larger project and you require some sort of formal authority to proceed.

The Outline Project Plan is a good way of bringing everything together. It should be set out in report format and needs to contain the following sections:

Background – why the project is taking place.

The objectives of the project – what it is aiming to achieve.

Any prerequisites – things that must be available for the project to begin or continue.

External dependencies – any outside agencies that may be involved as suppliers, partners or clients.

Planning assumptions – any assumptions you have made that could impact the project.

Project Gantt Chart – the summary level chart showing the main project stages.

Key deliverables – the tangible things that the project will produce or deliver.

Budget – the finance required to carry out the project in terms of real cost and nominal people cost (if relevant).

Resource requirements – the key people and any other resources that the project will need to be successful. This should include the percentage of their time they have to have available for the project.

One of the greatest problems in project management is not getting the key resources you need when you need them.

Even if you are not carrying out the project for anyone else, it's still a good idea to produce an Outline Plan.

This document forms the basis for agreement with your client, project sponsor, management, etc, and they will need to approve it for the project to continue. It is also a chance to show the project team what the project is about, and give them a chance to question and understand it.

Step 3 – Carry It Out

One of the greatest mistakes made on projects is to jump straight in and get started. If you've skipped steps 1 and 2, go back and do them!

If you've been through Step 1 (Define Your Objectives) and Step 2 (Developing Your Plan), then you know where you're going and you have a plan for how you're going to get there. You will also have obtained any business approval you need to continue. You can now start carrying the project out.

There is often business pressure to skip these initial steps, particularly on smaller projects. It might sound good sense to just get stuck straight in and not waste time but it should be resisted. Carrying out a project without having clearly defined objectives and a proper plan is like building a new type of bridge from A to B, without knowing exactly where A is, and the sure certainty that B will have moved by the time you get there.

Put simply, carrying out the project consists of allocating the necessary resources to the required tasks, tracking progress of the tasks until they are completed and measuring progress against your project milestones.

If only life were that simple the world would be a lovely place, but along comes Mr. Murphy:

Murphy's Law seems to apply doubly to IT projects and Channel Tunnels!

> # Murphy's 1st Law
>
> Whatever *can* go wrong
>
> *will* go wrong

So you also need to expect and to deal with problems. If you don't your project could rapidly get knocked off course. You can also benefit from the corollary to Murphy's First Law: If you plan on it going wrong it won't.

Saving Your Project

The chances are that, sooner or later, everyone who works with a computer will lose a large amount of work through a power cut or some other problem outside of their control. I have even heard of some people (not me of course) who caused the problem themselves!

So whenever you are working on a computer, save your work regularly. Microsoft Project is no exception to this rule. By saving your work you can try things out and always be able to get back to where you were. So save your project (and your sanity) by saving your work before (if you haven't already done so) and after making any major changes.

 You can also click File > Save on the Menu Bar.

1 To save your file (replacing the previous version) simply click the Save button 🖬 on the Toolbar.

2 If you want to preserve the previous version of the project click File > Save As from the Menu Bar. Enter the directory where you want to save the file and new file name and click Save.

3 The Project Planning Wizard appears to ask if you want to save the file with a baseline. The default is without, so leave it like that for now (see Setting a Baseline on page 113). Click OK.

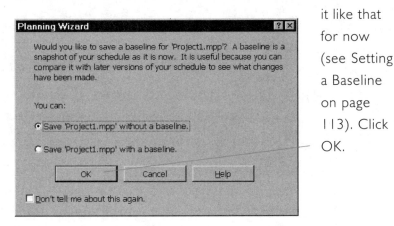

Step 4 – Hand It Over

Once the project is completed, the project manager's role is finished. But some project managers have problems with this final step.

First you have to let go and let the people who will be responsible for the on-going operation take over managing the process. They won't like it or feel comfortable if you are peering over their shoulders the whole time, so let them get on with it. You should have planned any required training and, once they are up to speed, they will be fine.

But, second, you cannot just dump the new process on them. As mentioned above, you should have planned any necessary training for them, but they will almost certainly have some problems adapting to new ways of doing things. What you must do is be available if they need you. This means scheduling some of your time to support the people doing the new process. This should only be for an initial, short critical period (usually around a month).

The hand over time is a great opportunity to finish off any outstanding paperwork or documentation. Tidy up the project files and back everything up.

The last scheduled task on the project should be to arrange and hold a post-implementation review. This is the time when you can go right back to the original objectives and see if they have been achieved or not. Was there anything that happened during the project that could not be dealt with or included in the project? If there was, should another project be initiated to deal with it?

As part of this review, the methods and tools used on the project should also be examined, and anything learnt should be noted for the benefit of future projects (your own, or those of anyone else in the organisation).

Last but not least, don't forget to thank everyone who helped in the project. They will appreciate it and you never know when you might want their help again...

Tasks and Milestones

Tasks represent the basic building blocks of a project and Milestones are the reference points we use to measure progress. In this chapter we will use these to form the basic project plan.

Chapter Three

Covers

Project Tasks

Project tasks are the basic building blocks of a project plan. They represent the pieces of work that have to be done in order to carry out the project.

A project could be treated as just one very large task, but there would be two problems with this:

1. It would be very difficult to estimate and schedule the effort required to carry it out. By breaking a project down into a number of smaller tasks, you will be able to estimate more accurately how long each will take and therefore how long the project will take in total.

2. It would be very difficult to control it and measure progress until the project was complete. By splitting it into Tasks you can track progress by the completion of individual Tasks.

So split your project down into Tasks that you can estimate, schedule and control.

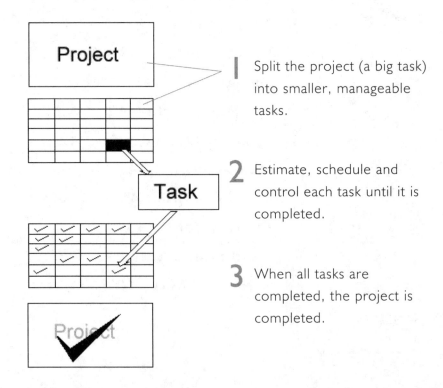

Project

Task

Project

1 Split the project (a big task) into smaller, manageable tasks.

2 Estimate, schedule and control each task until it is completed.

3 When all tasks are completed, the project is completed.

Creating a Task

Although you will need to build up all the Tasks involved in a project, it is very unlikely that you will be able to identify them all at the start. So to start with you should just put in any key tasks that you have identified.

Tasks can be entered in any view that includes Task Name, but the Gantt Chart view (which is the default view) is the easiest one to use to build up your Task list.

1 Open your project file and switch to Gantt Chart view (if you are not already in it).

2 Click on the Task Name field.

3 Type "Agree Project Objectives" and press **Enter**.

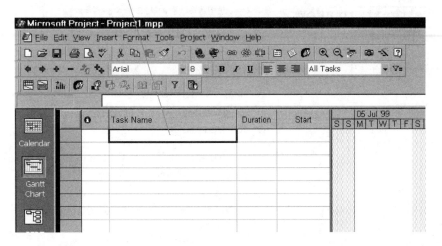

A Task ID is automatically assigned and the default task Duration of 1 day is allocated.

4 Click the Save button on the Toolbar and save the project without a baseline.

Task Duration

One of the main reasons for breaking a project down into Tasks is to be able to estimate the amount of work effort required to complete it.

While it is easier to estimate the work effort involved in a small piece of work than a large piece you may still not know what's involved. So what can you base your estimate on?

Experience – if you've done something similar before, how long did it take?

Advice – if you know someone who's done something similar, how long did it take them?

Guidelines – does your organisation have any guidelines available for you to use?

Guess – if none of the other options are available, your guess is probably as good as anyone else's!

Whatever method you use, get someone else to check it. Two heads really are better than one when it comes to estimating.

You can enter Task Duration as either Working Time (the default) or Elapsed Time. Working Time will be scheduled according to the Resources available while Elapsed Time will be scheduled on calendar days.

The bigger the task the more unknown factors there will be, so increase your estimate to allow for this.

Click on the Duration for Task 1 and use the spin controls to change the Duration.

For elapsed time type an 'e' in front of the type (em, eh, ed or ew).

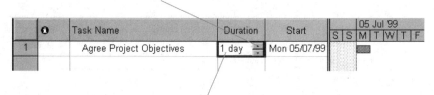

	❶	Task Name	Duration	Start	05 Jul '99 S S M T W T F
1		Agree Project Objectives	1 day	Mon 05/07/99	

2 To change the Duration Time Unit type the number of Units followed by **m** (min), **h** (hr), **d** (day), or **w** (wk).

Adding Tasks

To include additional Tasks at the end of an existing Task List, do the following:

1 Click on the first blank Task Name.

2 Type in "Identify Project Team", Tab to Duration, type "2d" and press Enter.

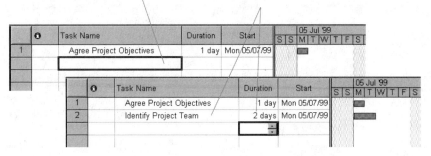

3 Now type in the following Tasks and Durations:

Produce Outline Project Plan	1d
Identify Business Case	2d
Analyse the Risks	1d

4 To insert a task into an existing task list, click the Task Name for Task 2 (Identify Project Team) and select Insert > New Task from the Menu Bar.

HANDY TIP

You can also use the Insert key as a short cut to insert a task.

	ⓘ	Task Name	Duration	Start	05 Jul 99 S S M T W T F S
1		Agree Project Objectives	1 day	Mon 05/07/99	
2					
3		Identify Project Team	2 days	Mon 05/07/99	
4		Produce Outline Project Plan	1 day	Mon 05/07/99	
5		Identify Business Case	2 days	Mon 05/07/99	
6		Analyse the Risks	1 day	Mon 05/07/99	

5 Type in "Identify Stakeholders", press **Enter** and Save your project.

Task Dependencies

When you first identify your key tasks you should sequence them in the order that they will need to happen.

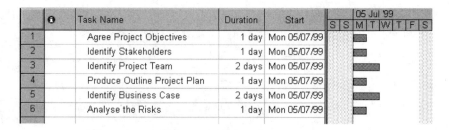

	ⓘ	Task Name	Duration	Start	05 Jul '99
					S S M T W T F S
1		Agree Project Objectives	1 day	Mon 05/07/99	
2		Identify Stakeholders	1 day	Mon 05/07/99	
3		Identify Project Team	2 days	Mon 05/07/99	
4		Produce Outline Project Plan	1 day	Mon 05/07/99	
5		Identify Business Case	2 days	Mon 05/07/99	
6		Analyse the Risks	1 day	Mon 05/07/99	

Very few tasks in a project happen in isolation. They are usually dependent on some input from other tasks and other tasks are usually dependent on them.

Typically, Task 3 cannot begin until Task 2 has been completed...

...and once Task 3 has been completed, Task 4 can begin.

In Microsoft Project you create these dependencies by linking tasks. Linking allows you to specify those circumstances where the start or finish of a task is dependent on the start or finish of another task.

The most common type of dependency or link is the finish-to-start dependency (as illustrated above) where the finish of Task 2 allows Task 3 to begin.

However there are three other types of link:

- Start-to-start, where Task 3 can start at the same time as Task 2.

- Finish-to-finish, where two tasks must finish at the same time.

- Start-to-finish, where the start of Task 3 marks the finish of Task 2.

But these are likely to be the exception rather than the rule.

Linking Tasks

Task dependencies are created by linking tasks.

The default dependency for linking tasks is a finish-to-start dependency and this will normally be the dependency you want for most tasks in a project. It is easiest to link all tasks this way to start with and then make any changes afterwards.

| Select all tasks in the project by clicking the Task Name column header.

HANDY TIP

You can also select tasks by dragging across the Task ID's or Task Names.

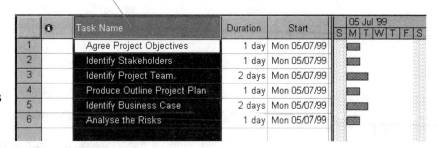

2 Click the Link Tasks button on the Toolbar: 🔗

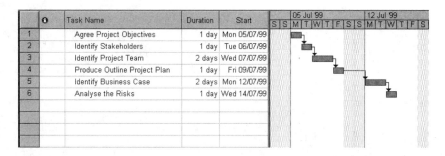

The tasks are all linked in a finish-to-start dependency.

You can select individual tasks to link by holding down **Ctrl** and clicking the individual Task Names or Task ID's.

3 Save your project without a baseline.

Un-linking Tasks

Once you have linked all the tasks in the project you may need to un-link some.

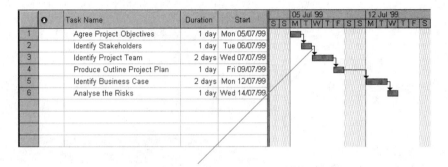

Double-click the link between task 2 (Identify Stakeholders) and task 3 (Identify Project Team). The Task Dependency dialog box opens.

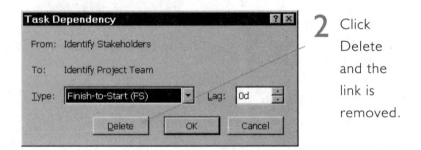

2 Click Delete and the link is removed.

To unlink several tasks you can also drag across the tasks to select them.

You can also un-link tasks by holding down Ctrl, clicking on the tasks and then clicking the un-link button on the Toolbar.

Changing Dependencies

Although the majority of tasks in a project will normally be in a finish-to-start dependency, you may need to change some to other types of dependencies.

1 Re-establish the dependency between task 2 (Identify Stakeholders) and task 3 (Identify Project Team) by selecting the tasks and clicking the Link Tasks button on the Toolbar.

2 Double-click the link between task 5 (Identify Business Case) and task 6 (Analyse the Risks) and the Task Dependency dialog box opens.

3 Click the arrow next to Type.

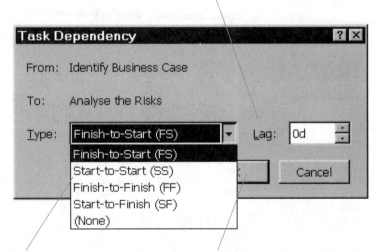

4 Select Start-to-Start and click OK. The tasks are now rescheduled to start on the same day.

	❶	Task Name	Duration	Start	05 Jul 99 S S M T W T F S	12 Jul 99 S S M T W T F S
1		Agree Project Objectives	1 day	Mon 05/07/99		
2		Identify Stakeholders	1 day	Tue 06/07/99		
3		Identify Project Team	2 days	Wed 07/07/99		
4		Produce Outline Project Plan	1 day	Fri 09/07/99		
5		Identify Business Case	2 days	Mon 12/07/99		
6		Analyse the Risks	1 day	Mon 12/07/99		

Moving a Task

If you need to move a task to a new position in the task list, the easiest way is to drag and drop by selecting the ID of the task (or tasks) you want to move and then dragging them to their new position.

Make sure you select the Task ID or you may only move the selected fields and not the whole task.

1 Click the Task ID for task 4 (Produce Outline Project Plan) to select it. Make sure you release the mouse button.

2 Now drag the task to after task 6 (Analyse the Risks). Notice the insertion point marker as you drag.

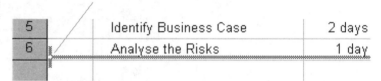

3 Release the mouse key. The task moves to its new position, its links are removed and the tasks are renumbered.

	❶	Task Name	Duration	Start	05 Jul 99	12 Jul 99
1		Agree Project Objectives	1 day	Mon 05/07/99		
2		Identify Stakeholders	1 day	Tue 06/07/99		
3		Identify Project Team	2 days	Wed 07/07/99		
4		Identify Business Case	2 days	Fri 09/07/99		
5		Analyse the Risks	1 day	Fri 09/07/99		
6		Produce Outline Project Plan	1 day	Mon 05/07/99		

4 Select tasks 4 and 6, click the Link Tasks button on the Toolbar and Save your project without a baseline.

Deleting a Task

If you need to delete a task from the task list, simply select it and delete it.

1 Select task 2 (Identify Stakeholders) by clicking on its Task ID.

	ⓘ	Task Name	Duration	Start	05 Jul 99 S S M T W T F S	12 Jul 99 S M T W T F S
1		Agree Project Objectives	1 day	Mon 05/07/99		
2		Identify Stakeholders	1 day	Tue 06/07/99		
3		Identify Project Team	2 days	Wed 07/07/99		
4		Identify Business Case	2 days	Fri 09/07/99		
5		Analyse the Risks	1 day	Fri 09/07/99		
6		Produce Outline Project Plan	1 day	Tue 13/07/99		

You can also use the Delete key to delete one or more selected tasks.

2 Click Edit > Delete Task on the Menu Bar. The task is removed from the project.

	ⓘ	Task Name	Duration	Start	05 Jul 99 S S M T W T F S	12 Jul 99 S M T W T F S
1		Agree Project Objectives	1 day	Mon 05/07/99		
2		Identify Project Team	2 days	Tue 06/07/99		
3		Identify Business Case	2 days	Thu 08/07/99		
4		Analyse the Risks	1 day	Thu 08/07/99		
5		Produce Outline Project Plan	1 day	Mon 12/07/99		

Microsoft Project only lets you undo the last action.

3 If you delete the wrong task (or tasks) in error you can always reverse your last action. Click on the Undo button on the Toolbar.

When you have used the Undo button it turns into the Redo button to allow you to cancel the Undo.

4 To redo whatever you have just corrected click the Redo button on the Toolbar.

The Redo button now turns back into the Undo button again.

5 Click the Undo button again to restore the deleted task (Identify Stakeholders) again.

The Task Form

Task Entry view is one of the additional views that is available in Microsoft Project. You can use it to view, enter and edit details of individual tasks.

REMEMBER

If the View Bar is not displayed you can get it back with View > View Bar on the Menu Bar.

| Click the down arrow on the View Bar until More Views appears.

2 Click More Views.

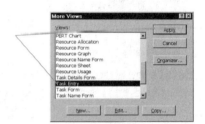

3 Scroll down through the More Views list, select Task Entry and click Apply. The Task Form is displayed in the bottom half of the view.

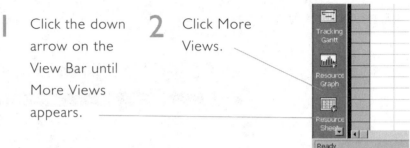

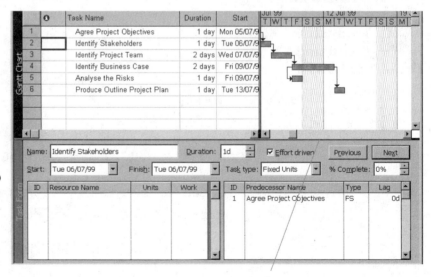

REMEMBER

You can drag the split bar up and down to change the size of the top and bottom panes.

4 You can now view, enter and edit task details directly. Double-click the split bar to change back to Gantt Chart view.

Project Milestones

Project Milestones are the key events that mark the progress of a project.

The simplest way of inserting a milestone is to enter a task with a zero duration.

1 Click on the blank Task Name below task 6 (Produce Outline Project Plan).

2 Type "Project Approval", press Tab, type "0" and press Enter. A milestone is inserted into the project plan.

3 Link task 6 (Produce Outline Project Plan) and task 7 (the milestone) by selecting them and clicking the Link Tasks button on the Toolbar.

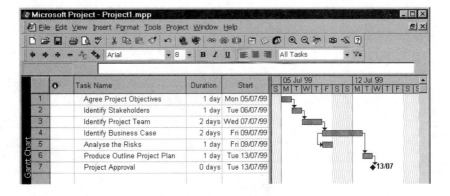

4 Click the Duration, type "5d" and double-click the task. The Task Information dialog box opens.

5 Click the Advanced tag, click the Mark Task as Milestone checkbox and click OK. The task changes back to a milestone but the duration stays as 5 days.

Recurring Tasks

Any task that is repeated within a project is called a recurring task. It could be a regular project team meeting, a review with your project sponsor or production of a monthly management report.

1 To insert a recurring task, click in an empty Task Name field.

2 Click Insert > Recurring Task on the Menu Bar and the Recurring Task Information box appears.

3 Type "Project Team Meeting;" type "1h;" select 'Weekly'; select 'Thursday'; and click OK.

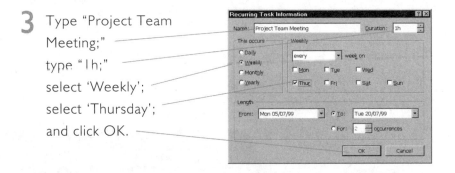

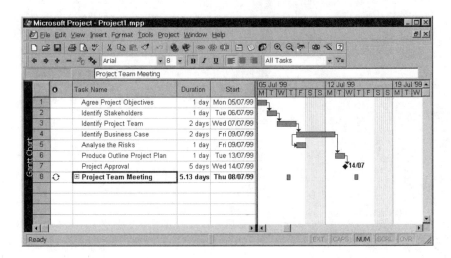

The recurring task is inserted. Click the "+" next to the Task Name to show the individual meetings.

Chapter Four

Adding Structure

In this chapter we begin to add some structure to the project by developing summary tasks and sub tasks and using outlining.

Project Structure

A simple project, like carrying out and presenting a strategy study, might consist of as little as a dozen tasks. A medium sized project, such as building a house or implementing a computer system could run into hundreds of individual tasks. A very large project could run into thousands of tasks.

If you try to identify and plan for every individual task right from the outset you will almost certainly be doomed to failure. In the early stages of a project there will usually be a large number of unknown factors. These factors will only become known as the project progresses. To cope with this you need to break a project down into manageable chunks one level at a time. This is usually represented in a hierarchical structure:

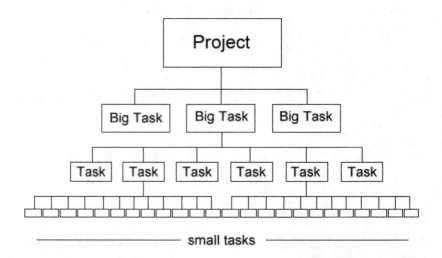

1 Break the project down into some discrete chunks (big tasks) with deliverables.

2 As you begin each big task, break it down into its individual tasks.

3 As you begin to work on each task, break it down into its individual sub-tasks (if relevant).

So when you first start a project you need to break it down into the first level major chunks (big tasks). Going back to our 4 step approach to carrying out a project we could use that as a basis for our big chunks. That would give us the following four steps as our first level big tasks:

1. Define the objectives

2. Plan the project

3. Carry it out

4. Hand it over

You would then start to identify the tasks required to carry out step 1 (defining the objectives) before worrying about the detailed tasks involved in step 2.

As you get towards the end of defining the objectives you would then start to identify and plan the detailed tasks in the next step (planning the project) and so on.

Working through the project in this manner means that there will be less unknown factors when you come to identify the tasks and estimate the effort involved in them.

In Microsoft Project the process of structuring your project plan in this way is called Outlining. The Outlining buttons are on the Formatting Toolbar when you are in Gantt Chart, Task Sheet and Task Usage views.

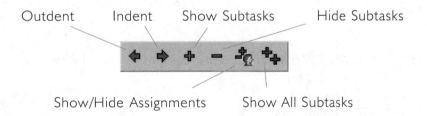

We will start to use these outlining features in the following sections.

Summary Tasks

A summary task is created just like any other task, but its subtasks are indented.

1 Click task 1 (Agree Project Objectives).

2 Click Insert > New Task on the Menu Bar (or press Insert).

3 Type the new Task Name "Define the Objectives" and press Enter.

4 Select tasks 2 to 8 by clicking and dragging their Task ID's and click the Indent button on the Toolbar.

	❶	Task Name	Duration	Start
1		⊟ **Define the Objectives**	**12 days**	**Mon 05/07/99**
2		Agree Project Objectives	1 day	Mon 05/07/99
3		Identify Stakeholders	1 day	Tue 06/07/99
4		Identify Project Team	2 days	Wed 07/07/99
5		Identify Business Case	2 days	Fri 09/07/99
6		Analyse the Risks	1 day	Fri 09/07/99
7		Produce Outline Project Pla	1 day	Tue 13/07/99
8		Project Approval	5 days	Wed 14/07/99
9	↻	⊞ **Project Team Meeting**	**5.13 days**	**Thu 08/07/99**

summary bar

These tasks have now become subtasks of task 1 (Define the Objectives) and are indented. Task 1 has become a summary task and is now shown in bold. It also has a summary bar in the right hand side of the screen (note it shows the 5 days for the milestone).

5 Now hide the subtasks and insert the other three steps and durations as shown below.

HANDY TIP

Hide sub-tasks by clicking the minus sign beside the summary task.

	❶	Task Name	Duration	Start
1		⊞ **Define the Objectives**	**12 days**	**Mon 05/07/99**
9		Plan the Project	10 days	Mon 05/07/99
10		Carry it Out	30 days	Mon 05/07/99
11		Hand it Over	15 days	Mon 05/07/99
12	↻	⊞ **Project Team Meeting**	**5.13 days**	**Thu 08/07/99**

6 Save your project without a baseline.

Changing the Time scale

Once you link the new summary tasks, they will go off the time scale in the right hand pane and you will not be able to see the whole project. However, this is easily remedied by using the Zoom in and Zoom Out buttons on the Toolbar.

1   Link the new summary tasks by selecting tasks 1 to 11 and clicking the Link Tasks button on the Toolbar.

2   Now use the Zoom In and Zoom Out buttons on the Toolbar until you have the whole project in view again.

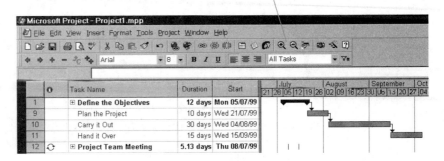

3   Now click on the Show All Subtasks button on the Toolbar and the Zoom In button to get back to the sub-task details.

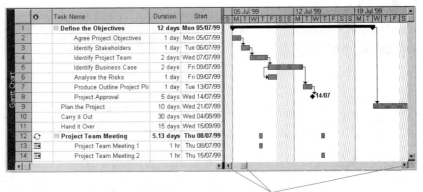

4   You may need to use the slider controls to bring the focus back to the required time period.

Project Stages

Conventionally in project management methodology, the first level summary tasks are referred to as project stages.

Project management methodology initially grew out of the construction industry and still retains some of that industry's terminology. In later years it has also been influenced by the software development industry which, interestingly, has a lot of similarities.

Using that influence, we can now build a little further on our four-step approach by expanding our second step (planning) into three separate stages:

- Determine what the business needs are.

- Define what we will need to do to achieve those needs.

- Work out how we are actually going to do it.

If this sounds a bit like 'overkill', keep an open mind for the time being. Hopefully you will begin to see why as we develop the process further. These six project stages are conventionally referred to as:

 Some people refer to these project stages as project phases.

1. Initiation – to define the project objectives and team structure

2. Strategy – to determine the business needs and payback

3. Analysis – to define what we will need to do

4. Design – to work out how we will actually do it

5. Build – to carry it out, make it, buy it, manage it

6. Implement – to hand over the new process

The chief benefit of this method is that the major expense or effort usually occurs in the Build stage. At each of the preceding stages you are able to reappraise the potential investment and ensure that it will still be of benefit. If it becomes questionable, the project can be wound up while costs and effort expended are still relatively low.

Implementing a 6-Stage Approach

While the 6-stage approach may indeed be overkill for a strategy study or a smaller project, somewhere between 4 and 6 stages will usually fit most projects. Just use whichever stages are appropriate to your project.

1 Select task 1 (Define the Objectives) and change the Task Name to "Initiation".

2 Select task 9 (Plan the Project), Insert a new task 9 "Strategy" and outdent it, then indent task 10 (Plan the Project).

3 Select task 11 (Carry it Out) and Insert three new tasks.
"Analysis"
"Design"
"Build" – then outdent them.

4 Select task 14 (Carry it Out) and Indent it.

5 Select task 15 (Hand it Over), insert a new task "Implement" and outdent it, then indent task 16 (Hand it Over).

6 Hide all subtasks by clicking the "-" beside any summary tasks and use Zoom Out on the Toolbar to get the whole project in view. It should look something like the following:

HANDY TIP

To insert more than one task, drag down the Task ID's to select the required number of tasks and press Insert.

	o	Task Name	Duration	Start	July 28 05 12 19 26	August 02 09 16 23 30	September 06 13 20 27	Oct 04
1		⊞ Initiation	12 days	Mon 05/07/99				
9		⊞ Strategy	10 days	Wed 21/07/99				
11		Analysis	1 day	Mon 05/07/99				
12		Design	1 day	Mon 05/07/99				
13		⊞ Build	30 days	Wed 04/08/99				
15		⊞ Implement	15 days	Wed 15/09/99				
17	↻	⊞ Project Team Meeting	5.13 days	Thu 08/07/99				

Although you have now implemented the six stage approach it still needs a little more doing to it. We will finish it off in the next section.

Contingency

When you first start a project you may be able to identify some of the key tasks but there will still be a lot of unknown factors, particularly in the later stages. To cope with this, and still be able to produce an outline schedule, you need to put in a contingency allowance.

How Much?

How much contingency should you add to cope with these unknown factors? How long is a piece of string?

While there is no right answer to this question, there is a rule of thumb that seems to work for me:

- add 100% to your initial estimate (yes, double it!)

- when you get to the end of the Strategy stage and estimate the remaining work on the project add 50%

- likewise at the end of the Analysis stage add 25%

- and finally at the end of the design stage add 10%

What you will be doing through the project is identifying more tasks. As you identify these additional tasks you can reduce your contingency allowance accordingly. Hopefully as you reach the end of each stage your contingency figure for that stage will be down to zero. It will have done its job.

Key Tasks

Before you put in your contingency figure it is a good idea to make sure you have identified any key tasks. Then you can put them in at the same time.

If the objective of the project was to select a new computer accounting package you would possibly have identified key tasks such as: Agree the Requirements; Select a Package; Purchase the Package; Install the Package; Train the Users; and Convert to the New Package.

Now let's put these key tasks and some contingency figures into our project.

Adding Contingency

Your project should currently look something like the screen shot on page 55.

1 Select tasks 1 to 15 and click Link Tasks on the Toolbar.

2 Select task 9 (Strategy), click Show Subtasks and change task 10 (Plan the Project) to "Contingency".

3 Insert 4 new tasks in front of task 12 (Design):

"Agree Requirements"   duration "5d"

"Select Package"   duration "5d"

"Purchase Package"   duration "2d"

"Contingency"   duration "3d"

Link them and indent them.

4 Insert "Contingency" under Design (10d) and indent it.
Insert "Install Package" (5d) under Build, change "Carry it Out" to "Contingency" (25d) and link them.
Under "Implement" insert "Train Users" (5d) and "Convert to New Package" (5d), change "Hand it Over" to "Contingency" (10d) and link them if necessary.

If you hide subtasks your project should now look something like this:

	0	Task Name	Duration	Start	
1		Initiation	12 days	Mon 05/07/99	
9		Strategy	10 days	Wed 21/07/99	
11		Analysis	15 days	Wed 04/08/99	
16		Design	10 days	Wed 25/08/99	
18		Build	30 days	Wed 08/09/99	
21		Implement	20 days	Wed 20/10/99	
25		Project Team Meeting	5.13 days	Thu 08/07/99	

5 Finally, double-click on "Project Team Meeting" and change the To Date to the end of the project (in our example 15/11/99).

Breaking Tasks Down

Having inserted summary tasks (Stages) as the first level of the project work breakdown, their constituent tasks become the second level. If you then need to break those tasks down into further subtasks they become the third level on the project work breakdown.

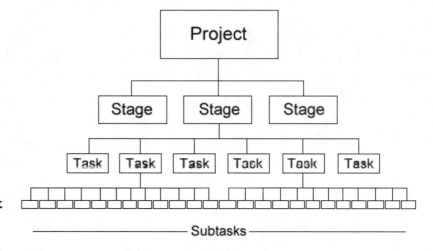

In project management method-ology, these third level subtasks are usually called Activities.

So how big or small should a task be?

If you are to be able to estimate, schedule and control a task with any degree of accuracy, it needs to be small enough to allow you to do this. But it must be large enough to have some form of deliverable or product so that its completion can be confirmed. Finally, although more than one person may work on a task, only one person must be responsible for its completion.

Conventional wisdom is that a task should be between 1 and 10 days effort (typically around 5 days). If it's bigger, then you should attempt to break it down into subtasks. If it's smaller, then see if you can combine it with some other task.

At the end of the day it's you, as the project manager, that should make the decisions, so these and any other guidelines are just that. If you want a 20 day task and it makes sense then have it, it's your project.

Outline Numbering

For a small project with a dozen or so tasks, the Task ID is probably a good enough way of keeping track of tasks. But as your project starts to build up you will want to be able to hide and show tasks and still keep track of where everything fits. Outline numbering allows you to achieve this.

1 Click Tools > Options on the Menu Bar. The Options dialog box opens.

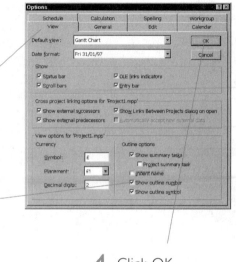

2 Make sure the View Tab is selected.

3 Check 'Show outline number' and un-check 'Indent name'.

4 Click OK.

5 Click Show Subtasks for task 1 (Initiation).

 HANDY TIP **If you don't want the +/- to show on summary tasks, un-check 'Show outline symbol' in the Options dialog box.**

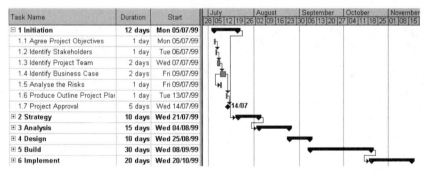

Task Name	Duration	Start
⊟ 1 Initiation	12 days	Mon 05/07/99
1.1 Agree Project Objectives	1 day	Mon 05/07/99
1.2 Identify Stakeholders	1 day	Tue 06/07/99
1.3 Identify Project Team	2 days	Wed 07/07/99
1.4 Identify Business Case	2 days	Fri 09/07/99
1.5 Analyse the Risks	1 day	Fri 09/07/99
1.6 Produce Outline Project Plan	1 day	Tue 13/07/99
1.7 Project Approval	5 days	Wed 14/07/99
⊞ 2 Strategy	10 days	Wed 21/07/99
⊞ 3 Analysis	15 days	Wed 04/08/99
⊞ 4 Design	10 days	Wed 25/08/99
⊞ 5 Build	30 days	Wed 08/09/99
⊞ 6 Implement	20 days	Wed 20/10/99

Your stages and tasks are now numbered in a structured format. Additional subtasks will be numbered 1.4.1, 1.4.2 and so on.

Subtasks

Any task that is larger than 10 days work effort will probably need to be split down into subtasks or the individual activities that make up the task. Even if a task is smaller than 10 days it may still be beneficial to split it down.

Activities

Third level subtasks are often referred to as Activities. They should be not less than 1/2 day and not more than 5 days and should be carried out by one person. For example if you have two people assigned to a task, it should be split into (at least) two subtasks or activities, each of which is allocated to one person.

By allocating these bottom level activities to one person it becomes easier to estimate, schedule and control them: easier to estimate as you can involve the person who will be doing it; easier to schedule as it involves only one person's time; and easier to control as you have only one person to ask about progress.

1 Open your project and show subtasks for stage 2 (Strategy).

2 Insert the 9 new tasks with their durations as shown and delete the old "Contingency" task.

3 Link the new tasks.

4 You decide that 2 people will carry out the interviews so insert 2 new tasks after 2.1 (Carry out Interviews).

Task Name	Duration
⊞ 1 Initiation	12 days
⊟ 2 Strategy	15 days
2.1 Carry out interviews	4 days
2.2 Produce draft requirements	2 days
2.3 Feedback sessions	1 day
2.4 Consolidate results	1 day
2.5 Finalise requirements	1 day
2.6 Evolve other recommendatior	1 day
2.7 Carry out risk analysis	2 days
2.8 Produce forward plan	1 day
2.9 Report to management	2 days
⊞ 3 Analysis	15 days
⊞ 4 Design	10 days
⊞ 5 Build	30 days
⊞ 6 Implement	20 days

⊟ 2 Strategy	15 days
2.1 Carry out interviews	4 days
2.2 Produce draft requirements	2 days

5 Type in the two new subtasks and their durations as shown (don't worry about the outline numbers).

⊟ **2 Strategy**	**15 days**
2.1 Carry out interviews	4 days
2.2 Interview Managers	2 days
2.3 Interview Staff	2 days
2.4 Produce draft requirements	2 days

6 Select the two subtasks and indent them.

Task Name	Duration	Start
⊞ 1 Initiation	12 days	Mon 05/07/99
⊟ 2 Strategy	15 days	Wed 21/07/99
⊟ 2.1 Carry out interviews	4 days	Wed 21/07/99
2.1.1 Interview Managers	2 days	Wed 21/07/99
2.1.2 Interview Staff	2 days	Fri 23/07/99
2.2 Produce draft requirements	2 days	Tue 27/07/99
2.3 Feedback sessions	1 day	Thu 29/07/99
2.4 Consolidate results	1 day	Fri 30/07/99
2.5 Finalise requirements	1 day	Mon 02/08/99
2.6 Evolve other recommendation	1 day	Tue 03/08/99
2.7 Carry out risk analysis	2 days	Wed 04/08/99
2.8 Produce forward plan	1 day	Fri 06/08/99
2.9 Report to management	2 days	Mon 09/08/99
⊞ 3 Analysis	15 days	Wed 11/08/99
⊞ 4 Design	10 days	Wed 01/09/99
⊞ 5 Build	30 days	Wed 15/09/99
⊞ 6 Implement	20 days	Wed 27/10/99

Notice that task 2.1 (Carry out Interviews) has now become a summary task (with a "-" beside it) and the two new subtasks are now numbered 2.1.1 and 2.1.2.

7 Hide the two new subtasks by clicking the "-" beside 2.1.

Task Name	Duration	Start
⊞ 1 Initiation	12 days	Mon 05/07/99
⊟ 2 Strategy	15 days	Wed 21/07/99
⊞ 2.1 Carry out interviews	4 days	Wed 21/07/99
2.2 Produce draft requirements	2 days	Tue 27/07/99
2.3 Feedback sessions	1 day	Thu 29/07/99
2.4 Consolidate results	1 day	Fri 30/07/99
2.5 Finalise requirements	1 day	Mon 02/08/99
2.6 Evolve other recommendation	1 day	Tue 03/08/99
2.7 Carry out risk analysis	2 days	Wed 04/08/99
2.8 Produce forward plan	1 day	Fri 06/08/99
2.9 Report to management	2 days	Mon 09/08/99
⊞ 3 Analysis	15 days	Wed 11/08/99
⊞ 4 Design	10 days	Wed 01/09/99
⊞ 5 Build	30 days	Wed 15/09/99
⊞ 6 Implement	20 days	Wed 27/10/99

Stages, Tasks and Activities

Summarising the content of this chapter, we have split a project down hierarchically into three levels: Stages, Tasks and Activities.

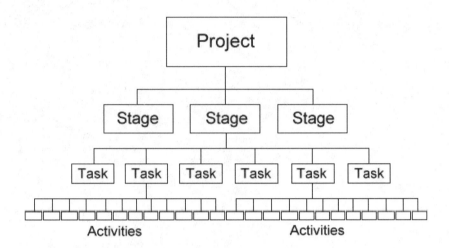

Stages

Stages are the first level summary tasks that define the structure of the project. The typical project will have around six of these main stages.

Tasks

Tasks are the basic building blocks of the project. Typically a task will be about 5 days work effort and it will have some sort of deliverable.

Activities

Activities are the third level (detailed subtasks) of a project. Larger tasks will be split down into activities to enable the project manager to allocate, schedule and control the work. Activities will still have some sort of deliverable but will be carried out by one person.

By structuring your project this way and reflecting it in your Microsoft Project plan you will be able to manage and communicate your project in the most effective way.

More About Tasks

This chapter goes into tasks in a little more detail. It covers lag and lead times, setting the critical path and splitting and moving tasks

Chapter Five

Lag Time and Lead Time

Up to now we have been linking tasks in a finish-to-start dependency with the next task starting immediately after the preceding task finishes. However, there are times when you want the tasks to overlap or have a gap between them.

Lag Time

Lag time is when there is a gap (or lag) between the finish of one task and the start of the next task.

Lead Time

Lead time is when there is an overlap between the finish of one task and the start of the next.

In Microsoft Project these are both specified using the Lag field (a positive number being lag time and a negative number being lead time).

> Show the sub-tasks in the Initiation stage of the project.

HANDY TIP

Use Zoom In and Out on the Toolbar to alter the time scale.

Task Name	Duration	Start	July 30 03 06 09 12 15 18 21
⊟ **1 Initiation**	**12 days**	**Mon 05/07/99**	
1.1 Agree Project Objectives	1 day	Mon 05/07/99	
1.2 Identify Stakeholders	1 day	Tue 06/07/99	
1.3 Identify Project Team	2 days	Wed 07/07/99	
1.4 Identify Business Case	2 days	Fri 09/07/99	
1.5 Analyse the Risks	1 day	Fri 09/07/99	
1.6 Produce Outline Project Plar	1 day	Tue 13/07/99	
1.7 Project Approval	5 days	Wed 14/07/99	◆14/07

Note that we set the Project Approval (milestone) with a 5 day duration to allow for the approval decision although there was not 5 days work involved.

2 Double-click the link between 1.6 (Produce Outline Plan) and 1.7 (Project Approval). The Task Dependency dialog box opens.

3 Change the Lag to 5d and click OK.

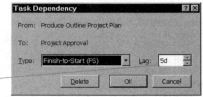

4 Change the Duration of 1.7 (Project Approval) back to zero.
   The schedule now shows the correct milestone date with
   the 5 day lag.

Task Name	Duration	Start	July 30 03 06 09 12 15 18 21 24 27
⊟ 1 Initiation	12 days	Mon 05/07/99	
1.1 Agree Project Objectives	1 day	Mon 05/07/99	
1.2 Identify Stakeholders	1 day	Tue 06/07/99	
1.3 Identify Project Team	2 days	Wed 07/07/99	
1.4 Identify Business Case	2 days	Fri 09/07/99	
1.5 Analyse the Risks	1 day	Fri 09/07/99	
1.6 Produce Outline Project Plan	1 day	Tue 13/07/99	
1.7 Project Approval	0 days	Tue 20/07/99	◆20/07

Now let's look at putting in lead time.

1 Double-click the link between 1.3 (Identify Project Team)
   and 1.4 (Identify Business Case) to open the Task
   Dependency dialog box.

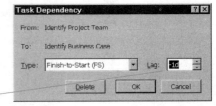

2 Click the down arrow
   spinner control to
   produce a Lag of "-1"
   and click OK.

Use Zoom In on the Toolbar to get the detailed time scale.

Task Name	Duration	Start	05 Jul 99 S M T W T F S	12 Jul 99 S M T W T F S	19 Jul 99 S M T W
⊟ 1 Initiation	11 days	Mon 05/07/99			
1.1 Agree Project Objectives	1 day	Mon 05/07/99			
1.2 Identify Stakeholders	1 day	Tue 06/07/99			
1.3 Identify Project Team	2 days	Wed 07/07/99			
1.4 Identify Business Case	2 days	Thu 08/07/99			
1.5 Analyse the Risks	1 day	Thu 08/07/99			
1.6 Produce Outline Project Plan	1 day	Mon 12/07/99			
1.7 Project Approval	0 days	Mon 19/07/99			◆19/07

There is now a 1 day overlap between 1.3 (Identify Project
Team) and 1.4 (Identify Business Case). We had already set
the link between 1.4 and 1.5 (Analyse the Risk) as a start-to-
start dependency so this task is now overlapped as well.

Adding Task Notes

You can add notes to a task in Gantt Chart view or any other Task view where the information box is displayed.

1 Open your project in Gantt Chart view.

2 Select task 1.6 (Produce Outline Project Plan).

3 Click the Task Note button on the Toolbar. The Task Information dialog box opens with the Notes tab selected.

4 Type in your note:
"Need to confirm report
format for the Outline
Plan" and click OK.

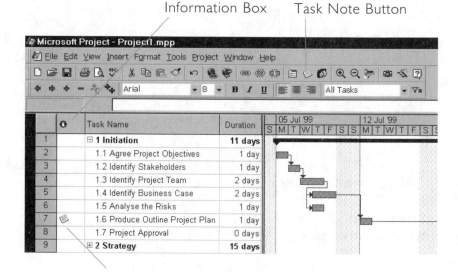

Information Box   Task Note Button

The Note Indicator is displayed in the
Information field for the task

HANDY TIP

Double-click the Note Indicator to edit the Note.

5 Pause the mouse pointer over the Note and the Note will pop-up on the screen.

Moving Around

As your project file starts to build up, you will not be able to get all the detailed information in one view at a time.

Scroll Bars

You can use the scroll bars to scroll the view horizontally and vertically. The Gantt Chart view has one vertical scroll bar which moves the task information and time scale in step. It also has two horizontal scroll bars so that you can move through the task information independently of the time scale.

HANDY TIP **Use the horizontal scroll bar slider and the task numbers are displayed in a pop-up box.**

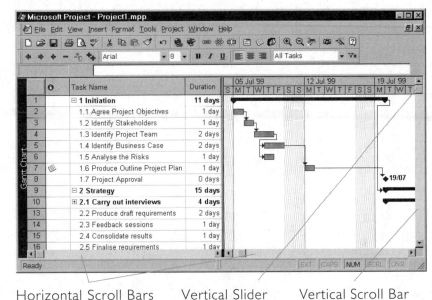

Horizontal Scroll Bars   Vertical Slider   Vertical Scroll Bar

Go To Selected Task

You can also use the Go To Selected Task button on the Toolbar to bring any task into view in the time scale.

1 Click on task 15 (Consolidate Results).

2 Click the Go To Selected Task button on the Toolbar. The time scale scrolls to the selected task.

The Critical Path

The Critical Path is the term given to the sequence of tasks that are critical to the duration of the project. A critical task is one that, if delayed or lengthened, will directly effect the project finish date.

Gantt Chart Wizard

The critical path is calculated by the Gantt Chart Wizard which will display the critical path tasks in red and non-critical path tasks in blue.

1 Click the Gantt Chart Wizard button.
The Wizard Step 1 dialog box appears.

2 Click Next and the Step 2 dialog appears.

3 Select 'Critical Path' and click Next.
The Step 9 (yes there's no mistake) dialog box appears.

4 Select 'Resources and Dates' and click Next.
The Step 13 dialog box appears.

5 Select 'Yes, please' to display links and click Next.
The Step 14 dialog box appears.

6 Click the 'Format It' button. The Step 15 (finished) dialog box appears.

7 Click the 'Exit Wizard' button. The Gantt Chart is now re-formatted.

Non-critical Task (blue)   Critical Path (red)

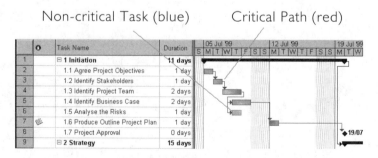

Splitting Tasks

Normally a task will be worked on from start to finish. However, a task can be split if it needs to be interrupted and finished at a later date.

We have a task 2.1.1 'Interview Managers'. If you were to discover that some of the managers were going to be away at a conference, you would need to reschedule part of this task for their return.

1 Select Task 11 (Interview Managers).

2 Click the Split Task button on the Toolbar. A screen pop-up asks you to select the split point.

3 Position the pointer in the middle of the Gantt bar for the task and click. The task is split and a gap of one day is opened.

4 Drag the right hand half of the task along to the next Monday and release it.

	ⓘ	Task Name	Duration	19 Jul 99	26 Jul 99
				S M T W T F S S	M T W T F S
7	📄	1.6 Produce Outline Project Plan	1 day		
8		1.7 Project Approval	0 days	◆19/07	
9		⊟ 2 Strategy	18 days		
10		⊟ 2.1 Carry out interviews	7 days		
11		2.1.1 Interview Managers	2 days		
12		2.1.2 Interview Staff	2 days		
13		2.2 Produce draft requirements	2 days		

The task is now split with a dotted line showing the link between the two halves and the project duration extended.

Moving Linked Tasks

When you split the task in the previous topic you left a gap in the Gantt chart. It would make sense to bring the following task (Interview Staff) forward to fill this gap.

⊟ **2.1 Carry out interviews**	**7 days**
2.1.1 Interview Managers	2 days
2.1.2 Interview Staff	2 days

1 Position the mouse pointer over the Interview Staff Gantt Chart bar. The pointer changes into a move pointer ⊕

2 Drag the task bar back to start after the first half of Interview Managers and release the key. A Planning Wizard appears telling you that the link cannot be honoured.

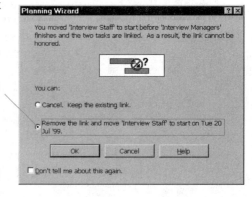

3 Select 'Remove the link' and click OK. The tasks are unlinked and a new critical path is established. Remove the link between 2.1.2 (Interview Staff) and 2.2 (Draft Requirements).

4 Ctrl+click 'Interview Managers' and 'Produce Draft Requirements' and click the Link Tasks button to re-establish the critical path. Move 'Interview Staff' back to start after the first half of 'Interview Managers'.

HANDY TIP

A calendar note has been added to the task saying when it starts as it is free standing.

0	Task Name	Duration
✎	1.6 Produce Outline Project Plan	1 day
	1.7 Project Approval	0 days
	⊟ 2 Strategy	16 days
	⊟ 2.1 Carry out interviews	5 days
	2.1.1 Interview Managers	2 days
📅	2.1.2 Interview Staff	2 days
	2.2 Produce draft requirements	2 days
	2.3 Feedback sessions	1 day
	2.4 Consolidate results	1 day

Resources

Up to now we have been looking at planning a project. This chapter introduces organising a project and working with project resources.

Covers

Chapter Six

Organising a Project

Organisation is a key area for a project manager. If you are not organised you will quickly lose track of what's happening on your project. The things you will need to organise on your project are the resources that you are going to use in order to complete the tasks and produce the deliverables.

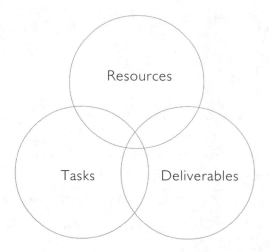

Resources

Resources represent the people and facilities that you will use on your project. As you have seen in the previous chapters, you can produce and schedule a project without assigning resources to it. In fact, if you are going to be doing all the work on a project yourself, you may not even bother to allocate resources (yourself) to the project. On the other hand if you are going to have other (non-project) work to deal with or if you are going to need other people and things on your project then you will be able to organise the project much better if you allocate resources.

In Microsoft Project you can store lots of information about the resources you will use on your project. Anything from availability to costs.

Fortunately, setting up resources and allocating them is very straight forward with Microsoft Project.

Project Stakeholders

The major resources on most projects will be people: the people who will be involved in the project; the people who will do the work. But there are also other people with a vested interest in the outcome of a project: people who will be impacted by it in some way. They could include your management, staff impacted by any changes and even your suppliers and customers. The generic term for all these people and groups is Project Stakeholders.

It is a good idea to start out by listing all your project stakeholders. You may not need to enter them all as resources but you should certainly keep the list available as you will probably need to think about communicating with them about the project from time to time.

So produce a list of your project stakeholders. Make sure you include:

- Your project sponsor or project board (whoever you report to on the project).

- Your project team (the people who will be working with you on completing the tasks).

- Any other people in the business who will be effected by the outcome of the project.

- Customers and suppliers (both internal and external) who will be effected by the outcome of the project.

- Anyone else who could be effected by the project.

When you have identified them all, think about the impact that they could have on your project. If they could have an impact in any way then you need to make sure you communicate what's happening on the project to them.

Remember that no-one likes being kept in the dark and you want them all on your side – not against you when the chips are down!

Allocating Resources

People who are assigned to a project are usually assigned on some form of temporary basis. That is, they will be working on your project for a set period of time. They will usually have other jobs and they may even have to keep on doing those other jobs for part of the time while they are also working on your project.

If you have someone allocated to your project for less than 50% of their time, you may find it hard to get them to prioritise project work over their other work.

If you have a person allocated to your project on anything less than a full-time basis you will need to take account of their other work commitments. This will sometimes be on the basis of their being allocated to the project for a certain number of days per week or month. Other times it might be on the basis of their being allocated to the project for a percentage of their time (typically 50–80%).

It will be very important to get a firm agreement on any part-time allocations up front, as you may need to fight for key resources at critical times. These are the sort of factors that need to be recorded as part of your project planning document.

The question you must ask yourself is how many days will a person work per week or per month on your project? If you know exactly when they will be available day-by-day then you can work that way. If not, you need some sort of rule to work to. Something that allows for them to be on holiday, on training courses, off sick, attending company meetings, etc. As a rule of thumb you could use the following:

There are 52 weeks in a year, less 5 weeks annual leave, less 2 weeks public holidays, less 1 weeks sickness, less 2 weeks training, less 2 weeks for other work-related things that will impact them.

Even this does not allow for people having those sort of 'unproductive days' that occur!

That leaves 40 weeks at 5 days a week or 200 days. If they are allocated to your project full-time you will get less than 4 days work a week from them. If they are not allocated full-time you will get proportionally less.

If you allocate people and schedule them on this basis (rather than 5 days a week) you will not get caught out in the resource trap.

The Resource Sheet

The first step in allocating resources is to enter your resources using the Resource Sheet.

HANDY TIP

You can also open it using View > Resource Sheet from the Menu Bar.

Open your project file and click the Resource Sheet on the View Bar. The Resource Sheet opens.

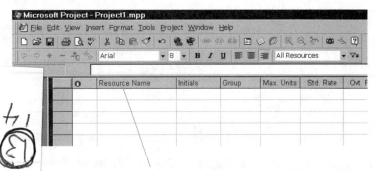

...k in the first Resource Name field, type your project ...ager's name and press Enter.

...w carry on typing in the names of the other people who ...be working on your project. You can also put in their ...als and group or department. Don't worry about the ...er columns for now.

0	Resource Name	Initials	Group	Max. Units	Std. Rate
	Prudence Project	PP	Proj Mgr	100%	£0.00/hr
	Joe Soap	JS	Marketing	100%	£0.00/hr
	Mary Dee	MD	Accounts	100%	£0.00/hr
	Wendy Page	WP	IT	100%	£0.00/hr
	Bill Buggs	WB	Director	100%	£0.00/hr
	Project Room	P	Facilities	100%	£0.00/hr
	Personal Computer	PC	Facilities	100%	£0.00/hr
	Board Room	B	Facilities	100%	£0.00/hr
	Overhead Projector	O	Facilities	100%	£0.00/hr

4 You can also enter other resources or facilities you will be using on the project.

Resource Information

In addition to the resource Sheet view there is also a Resource Information dialog box.

Select one of the Resource Names on the Resource Sheet and click the Resource Information button on the Toolbar.

The Resource Information dialog box opens.

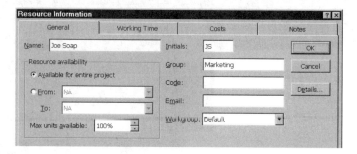

On the General Tab you can input and edit information for this resource. Make the following changes:

Available from: Wed 01/09/99
Max units available: 50% (click the down arrow)
Code: A209
Email: jsoap@bigco.com
Workgroup: Email and Web

Then Click OK.

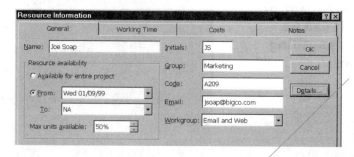

Click on the Details button to see the amount of additional information you can input.

Resource Notes

In the same way as you can attach notes to tasks, you can attach notes to a resource.

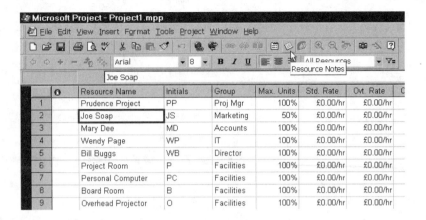

On the Resource Sheet select a Resource Name and click the Resource Notes button on the Toolbar. The Resource Information dialog box opens at the Notes tab.

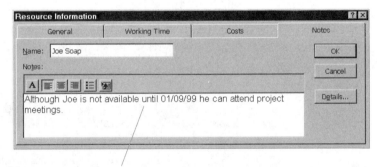

2 Type in your note and click OK. The Resource Sheet now shows a Note in the Information field.

If you hold the mouse pointer over the Note it will pop-up on the screen.

Assigning Resources

The process of allocating a resource to a task is called assigning.

1 Open your project in Gantt Chart view, select task 2 (Agree Project Objectives) and click the Assign Resources button on the Toolbar.
The Assign Resources dialog box appears.

Assign Resources

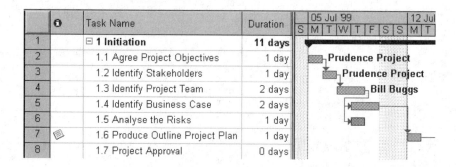

2 Select your project manager and click Assign.

3 Select task 3 (Identify Stakeholders) and assign your project manager.

4 Select task 4 (Identify Project Team), assign 'Bill Buggs' and click Close.

	ⓘ	Task Name	Duration
1		⊟ 1 Initiation	11 days
2		1.1 Agree Project Objectives	1 day
3		1.2 Identify Stakeholders	1 day
4		1.3 Identify Project Team	2 days
5		1.4 Identify Business Case	2 days
6		1.5 Analyse the Risks	1 day
7	🗐	1.6 Produce Outline Project Plan	1 day
8		1.7 Project Approval	0 days

The Gantt Chart now shows the assignments. Note that assignments are made at Units of 100% (the whole resource being allocated).

Multiple Resources

So far we have just assigned a single resource to each task (which is in fact the best way of controlling a project). However, sometimes you need to assign two or more people or other resources to a task.

1 Select task 5 (Identify Business Case) and click the Assign Resources button.

2 In the Assign Resources dialog box, click your project manager and click Assign.

3 Then click 'Bill Buggs' and click Assign. Your screen should look something like this:

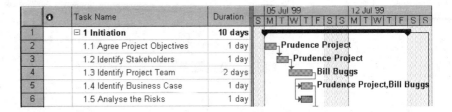

Note that both resources are now allocated to the task and that the duration has reduced to 1 day (2 resources x 1 days work = 2 days).

4 In order to keep the duration at 2 days, change the Units to 50% by clicking the down arrow in the Units field.

The task is rescheduled back to 2 days

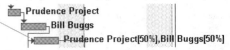

Multiple Tasks

As well as being able to assign multiple resources to a single task, you can also assign a single resource to multiple tasks.

1 Select task 6 (Analyse the Risks).

2 Hold down Ctrl, select task 7 (Produce Outline project Plan) and then select task 11 (Interview Managers).

3 Click the Assign Resources button on the Toolbar.

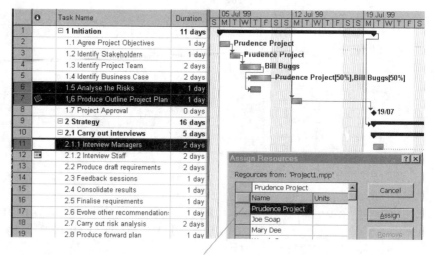

4 Select your project manager in the Assign Resources dialog box, click Assign and then Close.

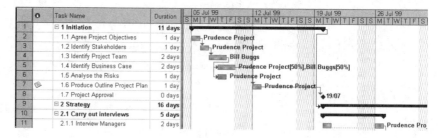

The three tasks are now all assigned to the selected resource.

Project Costs

In this chapter we look at adding costs to resources and tasks in order to build up the project budget and confirm (or reappraise) the business case for the project.

Chapter Seven

Project Budgets

If the first question a project manager gets asked is "When will the project be completed?" the second question is likely to be "How much will it cost?".

It is important to realise that until you have a full grasp of the requirements you cannot produce a reliable cost estimate for a project. Anything you do produce early on should be clearly labelled as a guess and issued with a corresponding 'health warning'!

Microsoft Project uses two types of costs: Resource Costs and Fixed Costs.

Resource Costs

Once you have identified all the products (deliverables), tasks and activities for a project, you will have the work effort required to carry out the project. This should include the appropriate element of contingency based on where you are in the project. By adding resource costs for all the people who will be working on the project, Microsoft Project will calculate the people-related costs for you.

If your organisation does not have an internal costing rate for people you can calculate one for yourself using twice their annual salary (to allow for overheads) divided by 190 (the rough number of productive days in a year).

Then you need to identify any external people costs such as consultants, auditors, etc.

Fixed Costs

Once you have the resource costs, you then need to identify any internal non-staff costs such as use of facilities, computer usage, etc.

Finally you will need to identify any other external capital or revenue costs such as software package purchase, software development, equipment purchase or lease costs and any other items of external expenditure.

All these costs can be input to Microsoft Project as Resource Costs or Fixed Costs on an appropriate task.

Resource Costs

Costs can be applied to resources or tasks. Typically you will use resource costs for people on the project. Costs are shown as an hourly rate which can represent their hourly pay rate or salary plus overheads or whatever standards you use for costing.

The easiest way to allocate costs to resources is through the Resource Sheet.

1   Open the Resource Sheet by clicking View > Resource Sheet on the Menu Bar.

HANDY TIP

If any resources are listed in red they are over allocated. (For how to resolve resource conflicts of this nature, see pages 106–108.)

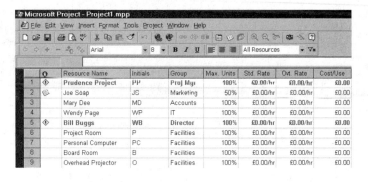

2   Enter the applicable standard hourly rates and overtime rates for the resources.

HANDY TIP

Although the default rate is hourly, you can input annual salary by adding a '/y' after it.

Resource Name	Initials	Group	Max. Units	Std. Rate	Ovt. Rate	Cost/Use
Prudence Project	PP	**Proj Mgr**	100%	£20.00/hr	£30.00/hr	£0.00
Joe Soap	JS	Marketing	50%	£25.00/hr	£37.50/hr	£0.00
Mary Dee	MD	Accounts	100%	£15.00/hr	£22.50/hr	£0.00
Wendy Page	WP	IT	100%	£20.00/hr	£30.00/hr	£0.00
Bill Buggs	**WB**	**Director**	100%	£40.00/hr	£40.00/hr	£0.00
Project Room	P	Facilities	100%	£0.00/hr	£0.00/hr	£0.00
Personal Computer	PC	Facilities	100%	£0.00/hr	£0.00/hr	£0.00
Board Room	B	Facilities	100%	£0.00/hr	£0.00/hr	£0.00
Overhead Projector	O	Facilities	100%	£0.00/hr	£0.00/hr	£10.00

3   Where a resource has a cost per use (such as the hire of an overhead projector) enter it in the Cost/Use field.

It is possible for a resource to have both an hourly rate and a per use cost. The per use cost being charged once each time it is used, and the hourly rate charged for the task duration.

Fixed Costs

Fixed costs are used where a task has a cost associated with it rather than the cost being associated with the resource. For example, task 24 (Purchase Package) will be the purchase cost of selected software.

1 Select the Gantt Chart view then click View > Table > Cost on the Menu Bar. The cost columns will be moved into the view replacing the entry columns.

2 Type in the estimated fixed cost for the relevant task.

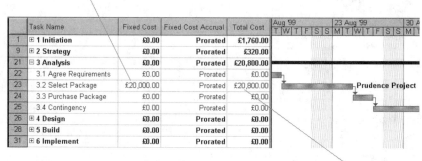

3 Select the task and assign the project manager to it. The total cost now includes the fixed cost and the resource cost.

Variable Resource Costs

During the life of a project it is quite possible that resource costs could change. For example, someone may receive a salary increase for doing such a good job on the project. Any cost changes should be entered through the Resource Information dialog box.

I In Resource Sheet view, select the project manager and click the Resource Information button on the Toolbar.

2 Click the Costs tab, click in the next Effective Date field and click the down arrow to get the calendar.

3 Select 1 September.

4 Type in the new standard and overtime rates and click OK.

HANDY TIP

For budget purposes you can use a percentage figure for an increase.

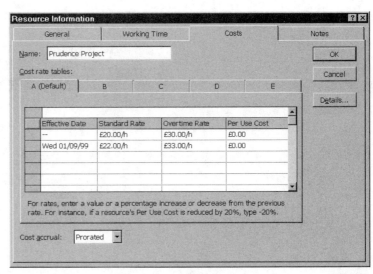

Cost Rate Tables

In addition to being able to change cost rates, Microsoft Project will also allow you to set up tables of rates for a resource. This can be useful if you need to use different rates for different types of work for the same person.

The cost rate tables are selected on the Costs tab in the Resource Information dialog box.

1 In Resource Sheet view, double-click Bill Buggs. The Resource Information dialog box opens.

2 Make sure the Costs tab is selected and click tab B in the Cost rate tables area.

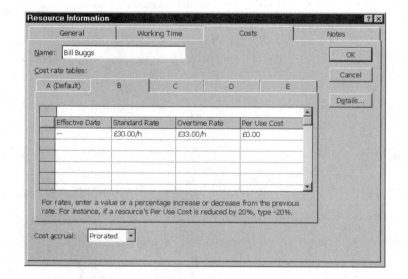

3 Type in the new standard rate '30' and new overtime rate '33'.

4 Click tab A and verify that the default rates have not changed.

5 Click OK to save the new rates table.

Applying Resource Rates

Having set up the new Cost rate table in the previous topic, we can now apply it to any tasks where it is relevant.

1 Select View > Task Usage on the Menu Bar.

2 Select task 5 (Identify Business Case), select Bill Buggs and click the Go To Selected Task button (this moves the time scale to bring the selected task into view).

3 Click the Assignment Information button. The Assignment Information dialog box opens.

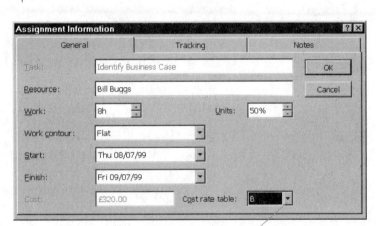

4 Click the Cost rate table down arrow and select table B.

5 Click OK. The new cost rate table is assigned to the task for Bill Buggs and the costs for the task is recalculated on that basis.

The Business Case

Once you have identified all the costs for the project, it is a good idea to re-examine the business case. The business case is the reason or justification for carrying out the project in the first place and once all the costs are known (or at least estimated) it may be that there is no longer a clear business case. If this is the situation the project should be reconsidered.

The project manager should not be responsible for making or supporting the business case. This is the responsibility of the project sponsor. The project manager's role is to determine the real costs of the project so that the business can make the decision about the viability (or not) of the project.

The costs for a properly planned project will normally start fairly low and gradually build up through the life of the project. Planning should take place at the start of the project so that a reasonable idea of the likely cost is available before too much time and expenditure has taken place. Then if the decision is made to cancel the project the costs will still be fairly low.

So what should the business case consist of? Basically, just a statement of the expected costs and benefits, defined as:

Project Costs – The costs of the project and any new systems implemented as a result of it over the number of years of expected life of the new systems. The new system could be a computer system or just a new way of working.

Project Benefits – The benefits (expressed over the same time period) would represent any savings as a result of replacing an old system plus any other quantifiable business benefits (such as new business revenue).

While the project manager should be responsible for the project costs, the benefits and the decision to go ahead with the project should be defined by the business or the project sponsor on behalf of the business.

Project Calendars

This chapter explains what the various project calendars are, how to create them, set them up for the project and assign and change them for individual resources.

Chapter Eight

Covers

Calendars

Scheduling a project consists of allocating tasks to resources in line with their availability. So before you can start scheduling you need to know the availability and non-availability of the resources you will be using – eg, if they are going to be on holiday or on a training course at any time during the project.

Microsoft Project uses calendars to determine working and non-working days, default start time and the working hours in a day.

So resources, tasks and availability (the resource calendar) are all interlinked. If any change happens to one of them it can impact on the others and on the project schedule.

There are two types of calendar: base calendars and individual resource calendars. Base calendars define the working days and hours for the whole project (or for a group of resources). Resource calendars define the working days and working hours for an individual resource.

HANDY TIP

There are two other base calendars provided: the night-shift and 24-hour calendars.

The standard calendar is the default project base calendar. It defines the working days and hours for the whole project. You can also create your own base calendars.

When a resource is added to a project, the standard calendar is allocated to that resource as its base calendar. Any changes made to the standard calendar are reflected in the resource calendars that are based on it.

The relationships between the various base calendars, the resource calendars and the project defaults require a little explanation.

If you consider them as three levels, they work like this:

1 Project Defaults are used by Microsoft Project to set the duration and work of tasks, and in the allocation of resources.

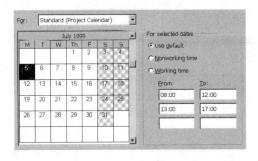

2 Base Calendars are used to define the working days and hours for the project (or a group of resources within the project). There are three base calendars provided: 1. Standard; 2. Night Shift; 3. 24-hour. You can also create your own base calendars.

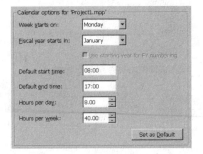

3 Resource Calendars are created for each resource and inherit their base calendar working days and hours. They are used to set any variations from the base calendar, such as annual holidays and meetings.

Project Defaults

Project defaults are initially set the same as the standard base calendar. Working time is Monday to Friday, 08:00 to 12:00 and 13:00 to 17:00 with no holidays.

Changes to the project defaults will not change base or resource calendars.

Changing the project defaults does not change any of the base calendars or the resource calendars based on them.

Changing the project defaults will change the way that tasks are allocated duration and the way that resources are allocated to them.

If you make any changes to the project defaults you must also change the relevant base calendar(s) to keep them in step.

You can also click Tools > Options and select the Calendar tab.

1 On the Menu Bar click Tools > Change Working Time. The Change Working Time dialog box opens.

2 Click Options. The Options dialog box opens at the Calendar tab.

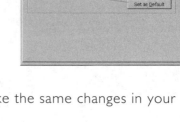

3 Make any required changes and click Set as Default.

4 If you have made any changes to the days or hours, make sure you make the same changes in your standard/base calendar.

Standard Calendar

 BEWARE

Changing the default settings will not change any base calendar.

The standard calendar has a default setting of 08:00 (8 am) to 17:00 (5 pm) for the working hours and Monday to Friday (with no holidays) for the working days.

The first step is to set up the base calendar for your project by making any required changes to the working hours and working days and putting in public or other holidays.

The Change Working Time dialog box is used to make these changes.

| Click Tools > Change Working Time on the Menu Bar. The Change Working Time dialog box appears.

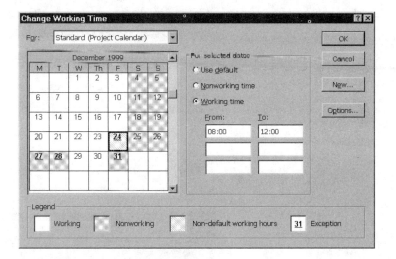

2 Change to August using the scroll bar, select Monday 30th and click Nonworking time.

3 Change to December, select the 24th, click Working time and then delete the afternoon working time. You do this by selecting the second From time and deleting it and then the second To time.

4 Now change the 27th, 28th and 31st to Nonworking time and click OK.

Creating a New Base Calendar

If none of the available base calendars fit the project requirements, or if you need a base calendar for a group of resources that work different hours, you can create a new one.

A new base calendar can be created from the project calendar defaults or by copying an existing base calendar. This will mean you don't have to redefine holidays, etc.

1 Open the Change Working Time dialog box and click New. The Create New Base Calendar dialog box opens.

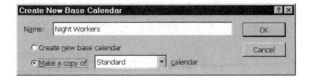

2 Type the name of the new base calendar as 'Night Workers', make sure 'Make a copy of Standard calendar' is selected and click OK. The new calendar is selected.

3 Select the day titles for T, W, Th and F by dragging across them. Then change the working hours to 00:00 to 05:00 and 21:00 to 00:00.

If you have people working shifts that span midnight (eg, 21:00 to 05:00) the hours before midnight have to be entered on one day and the hours after midnight on the next.

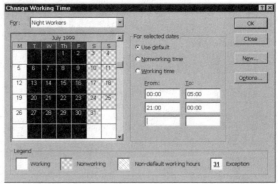

4 Change Monday to 21:00 to 00:00 and Saturday to 00:00 to 05:00. Click OK. You have set up your night workers base calendar.

Assigning a Calendar

If you create additional base calendars, they can then be assigned to the whole project or to individual or groups of resources.

The base calendar can be assigned on the Resource Sheet or in the Resource Information dialog box.

If you do not assign a base calendar, the standard calendar is assigned by default.

If changes have already been made to a resource calendar and a new base calendar is assigned to the resource, the changes will be retained and applied to the new base.

1 In Resource Sheet view double-click on Wendy Page.
The Resource Information dialog box opens.

2 Select the Working Time tab.
Note the Base Calendar is currently 'Standard'.

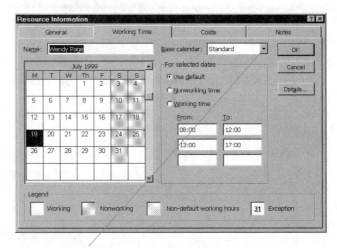

3 Click the Base calendar down arrow, select 'Night Workers' and click OK.

Resource Name	Initials	Group	Max. Units	Std. Rate	Ovt. Rate	Cost/Use	Accrue At	Base Calendar
Prudence Project	PP	**Proj Mgr**	100%	£20.00/hr	£30.00/hr	£0.00	Prorated	Standard
Joe Soap	JS	Marketing	50%	£25.00/hr	£37.50/hr	£0.00	Prorated	Standard
Mary Dee	MD	Accounts	100%	£15.00/hr	£22.50/hr	£0.00	Prorated	Standard
Wendy Page	WP	IT	100%	£20.00/hr	£30.00/hr	£0.00	Prorated	Night Workers
Bill Buggs	WB	**Director**	100%	£40.00/hr	£40.00/hr	£0.00	Prorated	Standard

Wendy Page is now working nights.

Changing a Resource Calendar

Each resource is automatically assigned a calendar based on the standard calendar unless a different base calendar is specified. However, while that should include the standard working days and hours for the project it will not include times that the resource is unavailable at meetings, on holiday or attending a training course.

1 Open your project and select Resource Sheet view.

2 Select 'Bill Buggs' and click the Resource Information button on the Toolbar.

3 Click the Working Time tab to display his resource calendar.

4 Use the scroll bar to move to August 1999.

5 Drag to select the middle two weeks.

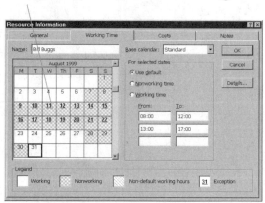

6 In 'For selected dates' select 'Nonworking time' then click on 31st August. The two weeks are now shaded to indicate nonworking time and underlined to indicate they are an exception.

7 Click OK and save the file without a baseline.

Project Scheduling

This chapter deals with scheduling a project and the affect of different task types on the scheduling process.

Chapter Nine

Scheduling

The process of scheduling uses the tasks, the resources allocated to them and their calendars to work out when tasks can be started, worked on and completed.

Forward Scheduling

The default approach to scheduling is to forward schedule from a start date. You can also backward schedule from a finish date.

The way that the schedule will be effected when resources, work effort or durations change is also dependent on the scheduling method and task types. The scheduling method can be either effort driven or not. Tasks can be one of fixed unit, fixed duration or fixed work.

Effort Driven Scheduling

This is the default scheduling method in Microsoft Project. In this method the duration of a task is adjusted to accommodate any changes to the resources. If a task is going to require 2 days work effort and you allocate two resources to it (at 100%), it will be given a duration of 1 day.

If you then remove one of the resources, the additional day's work will be reallocated to the remaining resource and the duration will be extended to 2 days.

You can turn effort driven scheduling off for a specific task or for all new tasks. When effort driven scheduling is turned off, adding an additional resource to a 2 day duration, fixed unit task will increase the work by 2 days and the duration will remain unchanged.

Task Types

The task type (fixed unit, fixed duration or fixed work) will determine what will be changed to accommodate any other changes.

The basic equation used by Microsoft Project is:

$$Work = Duration \times Units$$

Where Units are resources and their percentage allocation.

HANDY TIP

Work is the effort that will be required to complete a task; Duration is the length of time that it will take to complete a task; Units are the resources that will be used to complete a task.

Fixed Unit Tasks

The fixed unit task is the default task type in Microsoft Project. If resources are added or removed from a task, the duration is usually affected.

1 Click View > More Views from the Menu Bar, select Task Entry view and click Apply.

2 Select task 14 (Feedback sessions) and click the Assign Resources button on the Toolbar.

3 Click your project manager and click Assign.
Notice that 8 hours work has been allocated to Prudence.

4 Now assign Mary Dee to the task as well.
Notice that 4 hours work is now allocated to each of them and the duration has halved. Your screen should look something like the following:

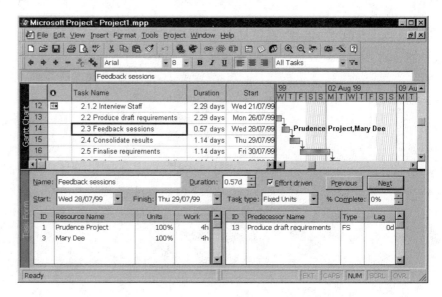

Most tasks will normally be fixed unit tasks and you will want to be able to change the duration by assigning more resources to a task.

Fixed Duration Tasks

If a task is a fixed duration task, then (as the name implies) the duration remains fixed whether resources are added or removed. This has an impact on the way that scheduling takes place, depending on whether effort driven scheduling is being used or not.

If effort driven scheduling is being used this means that adding another resource to an existing task will split the work between the two resources. The effort will remain the same, the duration will remain the same so their units will be reduced to 50% to balance.

If effort driven scheduling is not being used this means that adding another resource to an existing task will double the work. The duration stays the same, the units will be 100% so the work effort will double.

1   In Task Entry view, select task 17 (Evolve Other Recommendations).

2   In the bottom pane change the task type to fixed duration and de-select 'effort driven'.

3   In the top pane select task 17 again and click the Allocate Resources button on the Toolbar.

4   Allocate your project manager to the task (note at this time nothing has changed on the schedule).

5   Now assign Bill Buggs to the task. The bottom pane should look like the following.

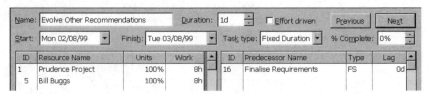

The duration has stayed the same (1 day), both people are allocated 100%, so the work effort has increased to 16 hours (2 days).

Fixed Work Tasks

The third task type is fixed work. A fixed work task must be effort driven so only the duration and resource units can be affected.

Adding another resource will reduce the duration and increasing the duration will reduce the resource units.

1   In Task Entry view, in the top pane select task 16 (Finalise Requirements).

2   In the bottom pane change the Task type to 'Fixed Work' and click OK.

3   Re-select the task in the top pane and assign your project manager to it (note the work effort is 8 hours).

4   Now assign Bill Buggs to it (note that the work effort is still 8 hours so the duration halves to 0.5 days).

5   Now change the duration back to 1 day and click OK. The resource units are both reduced to 50% so that the work effort remains at 8 hours.
     Your screen should look something like the following.

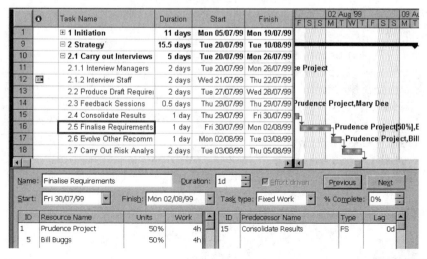

Contouring

When you assign a resource to a task, the total work is spread evenly throughout the duration of the task. This is referred to as a flat contour but there are a number of other contours that you can apply in Microsoft Project.

Contours can be applied or changed in Task Usage or Resource Usage views. In the former, the resources are grouped by task; in the latter, tasks are grouped by resource. In both cases the right hand side of the screen displays the work values and is used to contour the work.

Contours are applied using the Assignment Information dialog box. There are eight preset contours available:

Flat	Work hours are distributed evenly through the task duration.
Back Loaded	The hours start low and ramp up towards the end of the task.
Front Loaded	The hours start at 100% at the start of the task and tail off towards the end.
Double Peak	The hours peak twice during the task duration.
Early Peak	The hours peak at during the first quarter of the task duration.
Late Peak	The hours peak during the last quarter of the task duration.
Bell	The hours start and finish low and peak in the middle of the task duration.
Turtle	Similar to Bell but the hours start and finish higher (i.e. there is less variation).

HANDY TIP

You can see the percentages that will be used by the different contours in Work Contour field (assignment field) from the Help Index.

Once a contour has been applied to a task, any changes to the task start or finish dates, the resources allocated or the duration will be applied using the contour.

...cont'd

HANDY TIP You can drag the heading dividers to increase or decrease the width of a field.

1 In Resource Usage view select Analyse the Risks (one of your project manager's tasks).

2 Click the Go To Selected Task button on the Toolbar to bring the task into view.

3 Click in the Work field and increase the work to 11 hours (8 hours on the first day and 3 on the second).

4 Click the Assignment Information button on the Toolbar. The Assignment Information dialog box opens.

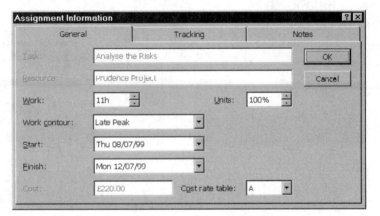

5 Click the Work contour down arrow and change the Work contour to Late Peak. The work contour changes and a contour indicator is added.

❶	Resource Name	Work	Details	T	F	S	S	12 Jul 99 M
◈	⊟ Prudence Project	115 hrs	Work	5.8h	9.95h			5.25h
	Agree Project Objective	8 hrs	Work					
	Identify Stakeholders	8 hrs	Work					
	Identify Business Case	8 hrs	Work	4h	4h			
⏵⏸	Analyse the Risks	11 hrs	Work	1.8h	5.95h			3.25h
	Produce Outline Project	8 hrs	Work					2h
🖉	Interview Managers	16 hrs	Work					
	Feedback Sessions	4 hrs	Work					
	Finalise Requirements	4 hrs	Work					
	Evolve Other Recomme	8 hrs	Work					
	Select Package	40 hrs	Work					

6 Save your file then try applying different contours to see the affect.

Forward and Back Scheduling

The default method of scheduling is forward scheduling from the project start date. This is what we have been using so far. However, there are some times when you have to complete a project by a certain date. By scheduling backwards from a finish date you can see when a project has to start.

If you haven't already done so, save your project now.

It is good practice to save your project before making any major changes to it. Just in case!

1 In Gantt Chart view, hide all sub-tasks and zoom out to get the whole project in view.

2 Click Project > Project Information on the Menu Bar.

3 Change the 'Schedule from' to 'Project Finish Date'. Note that the schedule stays the same as it has used the existing Finish date.

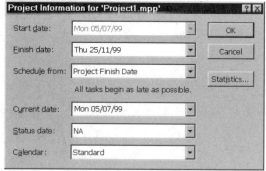

4 Now change the Finish date to a later date (31 March 2000) and the project is rescheduled.

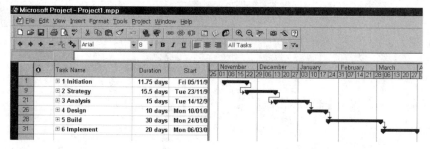

5 Use Save As to save this project file using a different name as we won't be using it again.

Conflicts and Constraints

This chapter deals with resource conflicts, manual and automatic levelling and the use of task constraints. It also introduces setting a baseline and saving interim plans.

Chapter Ten

Resource Conflicts

As you begin to assign resources to tasks and then make subsequent changes to tasks and schedules, you will begin to get resource conflicts.

A resource conflict is where a resource is scheduled to perform more work than they can carry out in the time available. Microsoft Project flags these conflicts for you by highlighting the relevant resource information in red and displaying a levelling indicator. Once these conflicts are identified the schedule needs to be examined and a decision made on how to resolve the conflict.

You can resolve these conflicts manually using Microsoft Project scheduling or you can let Microsoft Project automatically adjust the schedule by changing resources or task assignments for you.

1   Open your project file in Resource Sheet view.
    The over allocated resources are highlighted in red and have a levelling indicator.

	ⓘ	Resource Name	Initials	Group	Max. Units	Std. Rate	Ovt. Rate	Cost/Use
1	◈	**Prudence Project**	PP	Proj Mgr	100%	£20.00/hr	£30.00/hr	£0.00
2	✍	Joe Soap	JS	Marketing	50%	£25.00/hr	£37.50/hr	£0.00
3		Mary Dee	MD	Accounts	100%	£15.00/hr	£22.50/hr	£0.00
4		Wendy Page	WP	IT	100%	£20.00/hr	£30.00/hr	£0.00
5	◈	**Bill Buggs**	WB	Director	100%	£40.00/hr	£40.00/hr	£0.00
6		Project Room	P	Facilities	100%	£0.00/hr	£0.00/hr	£0.00
7		Personal Computer	PC	Facilities	100%	£0.00/hr	£0.00/hr	£0.00
8		Board Room	B	Facilities	100%	£0.00/hr	£0.00/hr	£0.00
9		Overhead Projector	O	Facilities	100%	£0.00/hr	£0.00/hr	£10.00

2   Click View > Toolbar > Resource Management to open the Resource Management Toolbar.

3   Click the Resource Allocation view button and then the Go To Next Over allocation button on the Resource Management Toolbar.

4   Click the Go To Next Over allocation button again to go to the next over allocation.

Resource Levelling

Resource conflicts can be resolved manually or automatically. The process used by Microsoft Project to resolve conflicts is termed 'levelling'.

The Resource Levelling dialog box is used to carry out levelling adjustments.

HANDY TIP

Always save your project before levelling. Then if anything goes wrong you can get back to where you were.

1   In Resource Allocation view, click Project > Project Information on the Menu Bar.
    Note the current finish date (25/11/99) and click Cancel.

2   Select the lower (Levelling Gantt) pane so it is active.

3   Click Tools > Resource Levelling on the Menu Bar.
    The Resource Levelling dialog box opens.

4   Check that the default options are selected as in the screen shot to the right.

5   Click 'Level Now' to level the project.
    The conflict between tasks 5 (Identify the Business Case) and 6 (Analyse the Risks) has been resolved by splitting task 6 (Analyse the Risks) and adjusting some other tasks.

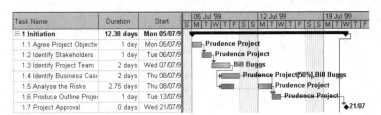

6   Click Project > Project Information on the Menu Bar.
    Note the finish date is still 25/11/99. The project has been levelled without any slippage.

Manual Adjustments

In addition to using automatic resource levelling you can also resolve conflicts manually. In fact, you sometimes need to make manual adjustments to stop Microsoft Project from automatically extending the schedule if it is unacceptable.

To manually resolve a conflict you will need to take steps such as the following:

- Allocate more resources to a task.

- Reschedule or split a task.

- Add overtime working.

- Reallocate tasks to a different resource.

1 First go through your project and allocate your project manager as the resource for all unallocated tasks.

2 Click the Resource Allocation view button and then the Go To Next Over allocation button on the Resource Management Toolbar.
Tasks 11 (Interview Managers) and 12 (Interview Staff) are causing the over allocation.

The Assign Resources button is exactly the same as the one on the Standard Toolbar.

3 Change into Gantt Chart view, select task 12 (Interview Staff) and click the Assign Resources button on the Resource Management Toolbar.

4 Click Replace (to replace the current resource), select Mary Dee, click OK and click Close.

5 Switch to Resource Allocation view and then click the Go To Next Over allocation button.
By reallocating the task to a different resource you have removed the over allocation and resolved the conflict manually.

Task Constraints

When tasks are first entered into a project they have the project start date as their start date. As they are linked and have resources assigned to them, they will be scheduled depending on their dependencies and resource availability and be given their own start and finish dates.

Sometimes these allocated start and finish dates are not viable in the real world and a start or finish date has to be imposed. When this happens it is setting a task constraint.

Task constraints are set in the form of start/finish on (or near) a particular date, no earlier/later than a particular date, or as soon/late as possible. The default constraint on a forward scheduled project is As Soon As Possible and this is applied to all tasks. For backward scheduled projects the default constraint is As Late As Possible.

Too many constraints will make it difficult to resolve schedule conflicts.

Constraints can be flexible or inflexible. A flexible constraint is one where the project finish date can be moved by the task. An inflexible constraint is one where the project finish date cannot be moved by the task. The following table lists the constraint types and whether they are flexible:

Constraint	Flexible for
As Soon As Possible	All projects
As Late As Possible	All projects
Finish No Earlier Than	Forward scheduled projects
Start No Earlier Than	Forward scheduled projects
Finish No Later Than	Backward scheduled projects
Start No Later Than	Backward scheduled projects

The first two constraints do not use a date, the others have a date associated with them. The date is the earliest or latest date that the task can start or finish (as appropriate to the constraint).

Applying Constraints

The usual reason for applying a constraint to a task is that some internal or external factor means it can only happen at a particular time.

For example if you did not want to start using a new accounting package until the start of the new year (1 January) you might well want to set a 'Start No Earlier Than' constraint.

1 In Gantt Chart view select task 33 (Convert to New Package) and click the Go To Selected Task button.

2 Double-click the task and the Task Information dialog box opens.

3 Select the General tab and note the current start and finish dates for the task.

4 Click the Advanced tab, select the 'Start No Earlier Than' constraint and select the date as 1 January 2000.

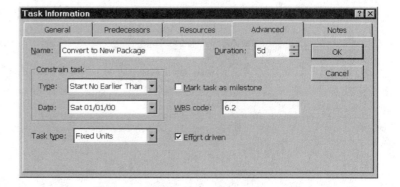

5 Click OK. The constraint is set, the schedule adjusted and an indicator added.

Constraint Conflicts

If you set a constraint that causes a conflict, the Planning Wizard appears to warn you of the problem and offer suggestions where appropriate.

1   Save your project, then, in Gantt Chart view double-click on task 20 (Report to Management).
The Task Information dialog box opens.

2   Click the General tab and note the current finish date.

3   Click the Advanced tab and select 'Must Finish On' as the constraint.

4   Select the previous Friday's date (06/08/99) and click OK. The Planning Wizard dialog box opens warning you of the scheduling conflict that could occur if you go ahead and set the constraint.

Planning Wizard

You set a Must Finish On constraint on the task 'Report to Management'. This could result in a scheduling conflict either now or later because this task has at least one other task linked to it.

You can:

(•) Cancel. No constraint will be set on 'Report to Management'.

( ) Continue, but avoid the conflict by using a Finish No Earlier Than constraint instead.

( ) Continue. A Must Finish On constraint will be set.

[OK]   [Cancel]   [Help]

☐ Don't tell me about this again.

BEWARE

Do not do this unless you have saved your project first.

5   Normally you should cancel. As long as you have saved your project file, select Continue and click OK.
You will get a further scheduling conflict warning. If you still continue the schedule will be updated but task 20 needs to start before tasks 18 and 19 are completed!

Viewing Constraints

When a task has a constraint applied in Microsoft Project there will be an indicator present. If you pause your cursor over it a pop-up will display details of the constraint. In addition, a flexible constraint will have a blue dot and an inflexible constraint a red dot.

You can also view constraints using the Constraints Date Table.

1 Open your project in Gantt Chart view and pause your cursor over the indicator on task 20 (Report to Management) which has a red dot so it is an inflexible constraint. The constraint details appear in a pop-up box.

2 Do the same for task 33 (Convert to New Package) which has a blue dot.

3 Select View > More Views > Task Sheet from the Menu Bar and then click Apply.

4 Select View > Table > More Tables from the Menu Bar. The More Tables dialog box appears.

5 Select Constraint Dates and click Apply. The Constraint Dates Table is displayed.

	Task Name	Duration	Constraint Type	Constraint Date
1	⊞ Initiation	12.38 days	As Soon As Possible	NA
9	⊟ Strategy	13.63 days	As Soon As Possible	NA
10	⊞ Carry out Interviews	5 days	As Soon As Possible	NA
13	Produce Draft Requirements	2 days	As Soon As Possible	NA
14	Feedback Sessions	0.5 days	As Soon As Possible	NA
15	Consolidate Results	1 day	As Soon As Possible	NA
16	Finalise Requirements	1 day	As Soon As Possible	NA
17	Evolve Other Recommendations	1 day	As Soon As Possible	NA
18	Carry Out Risk Analysis	2 days	As Soon As Possible	NA
19	Produce Forward Plan	1 day	As Soon As Possible	NA
20	Report to Management	2 days	Must Start On	Fri 06/08/99
21	⊞ Analysis	15 days	As Soon As Possible	NA
26	⊞ Design	10 days	As Soon As Possible	NA
28	⊞ Build	30 days	As Soon As Possible	NA
31	⊟ Implement	59.5 days	As Soon As Possible	NA
32	Train Users	5 days	As Soon As Possible	NA
33	Convert to New Package	5 days	Start No Earlier Than	Sat 01/01/00
34	Contingency	10 days	As Soon As Possible	NA

Setting a Baseline

Once you have created your project plan, allocated resources, resolved any conflicts and are happy with the project schedule, you are ready to set a baseline.

The baseline represents a record of a set point in time where you have agreed and fixed your project plan.

HANDY TIP

If you accidentally set a baseline too soon you can replace the earlier baseline.

That is not to say that things won't change during the project – they undoubtedly will – but you will then be able to compare how things actually worked out with how they were planned.

When you set a baseline the dates, times and other information about all the tasks is recorded.

1 Open your project in Gantt Chart view.

2 Select Tools > Tracking > Save Baseline from the Menu Bar. The Save Baseline dialog box opens.

3 Select the 'Save baseline' and 'For Entire project' options.

4 Click OK. The project is now baselined.

5 Select Project > Project Information from the Menu Bar. Then click Statistics on the dialog box. This shows the current, baseline and actual details for the project.

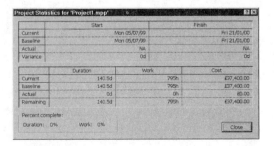

Interim Plans

As well as setting a baseline (which should be retained throughout the project) you can also create up to ten interim plans during the project.

You may wish to create new interim plans at the end of each project stage to reflect any changes to the project that have been agreed. Or you may wish to produce interim plans to reflect possible changes to the project.

For longer projects it will be particularly useful as things do change with time and the use of interim plans will enable you to backtrack to where the project changed direction.

Interim plans hold start and finish dates for each task.

1 Select Tools > Tracking > Save Baseline from the Menu Bar. The Save Baseline dialog box appears.

2 Select 'Save Interim plan'; 'Copy: Start/Finish'; 'Into: Start1/Finish1'; 'For: Entire project'; and click OK.

3 As your project progresses you can copy into Start2/Finish2 and so on.

4 You can also update interim plans by copying over a previous interim plan in 'Copy Into'.

At the end of the project you will be able to look back at the interim plans as well as the original baseline as part of your post implementation review.

Printing Reports

This chapter covers the set up, preview and printing of charts and reports. It introduces filtering and sorting of data to enable views and reports to be tailored to specific project requirements.

Chapter Eleven

Covers

Printing

If your project is going to be successful you will need to communicate information on the project and its progress on a regular basis. In addition to the 26 pre-defined views (which you can print), Microsoft Project also contains an additional 25 pre-defined report formats for printing information about your project.

Although the printed project Gantt chart is a very useful tool for communicating basic project progress information, different groups of people will need information presented to them in different ways.

The project team will need detailed information on the current stage, tasks and activities and their progress against schedule. They will also need to see the 'big picture' from time to time so that they don't lose sight of the overall project.

Management will usually only require information at the summary level together with details of what problems and issues have occurred, or perhaps might occur.

When faced with choices (such as 'do we increase the scope of the project to include this new area we have uncovered or do we stick with the original schedule?') you can produce reports that show the answers to the 'what if' type of questions.

The types of report that can be produced are as follows:

Any chart view (using Print from the Toolbar).

Overviews (summary, top-level and critical tasks).

Current Activities (tasks due, in progress or slipping).

Cost, Assignment, Workload or Custom reports.

The Page Setup dialog box allows you to set the page orientation (portrait or landscape), adjust margin widths, change scales, create headers and footers and control the flow of information.

Headers and Footers

In addition to the basic information displayed in a report, Microsoft Project allows you to create your own headers and footers which are displayed at the top and bottom of every page in a report. These are set up using the Page Setup dialog box.

You can enter any text you like and also include any of the following system and project information:

Page Number, Total Page Count, Project Title, Company Name, Manager Name, Project Start Date, Project Finish Date, Project Current Date, Project Status Date, View Name, Report Name, Filter Name, File Name, Last Saved Date, System Date, System Time, Subject, Author, Keyword.

1   Open your project in Gantt Chart view and hide all sub-projects.

2   Select File > Page Setup from the Menu Bar (to open the Page Setup dialog box) and click the Header tab.

3   Click the Alignment: Center tab and then click in the text area below it.

4   Click the down arrow next to 'Page Number', select 'Company Name' and click Add. Type a space then select 'Project Title' and click Add.

You can click Print Preview to see how it looks (see next topic).

5   Now click the Footer tab and add the 'Total Page Count' after the page number (put " of " between them) and click OK to save the header and footer information.

Previewing Reports

With Microsoft Project it is always a good idea to preview a report before printing it. That way you can make sure it will look the way you want, and make any final adjustments to it.

1 Open your project in Gantt Chart view with all sub-tasks hidden.

2 Click Print Preview on the Toolbar. Print Preview opens and should look something like this:

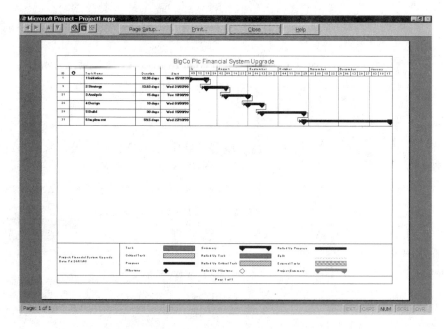

 You can always print your current chart view using the Print button.

3 If you move your cursor over the preview page it changes to a magnifying glass which allows you to zoom in and out.

4 Zoom in and check your header and footer. You can use Page Setup to change any details (such as the font size). Click Close to exit Print Preview.

Printing Reports

There are 25 pre-defined report formats available in Microsoft Project.

1 Select View > Reports from the Menu Bar. The Reports dialog box opens.

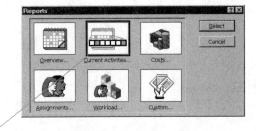

HANDY TIP

You can also just double-click on Current Activities.

2 Click on Current Activities and Select. The Current Activity Reports dialog box opens.

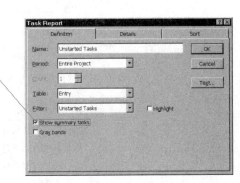

3 Select 'Unstarted Tasks' and click Edit. The Task Report dialog box opens.

4 On the Definition tab select 'Show summary tasks'.
On the Details tab select 'Assignment Notes'.
Click OK.

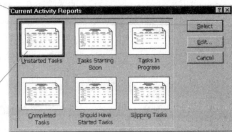

HANDY TIP

Using these steps and print preview you can explore all the report formats available without needing to print.

5 Click Select on the Current Activity Reports dialog box. The report is previewed.

6 Click Print and then OK to print the report. The report is printed and you are returned to the Reports dialog box. Click Cancel to close Reports.

Report Filters

In addition to its report printing capabilities, Microsoft Project also allows you to filter and sort data before printing it. Filtering allows you to select just the information that you wish to be displayed.

There are a number of pre-defined filters that you can use to select things such as late tasks, tasks in progress, work that is over budget, and so on. Microsoft Project actually contains 30 pre-defined task filters and 21 pre-defined resource filters. In addition you can also create your own custom filters to meet the specific requirements of your project.

Filters can be used to focus on specific tasks in your project or on specific resources in the project. When you apply a filter only the tasks or resources that meet the filter criteria are displayed. All other tasks and resources are hidden while you are using a filter.

Applying filters to your project does not change the data in any way, it just changes the way you are viewing it.

Microsoft Project contains an AutoFilter feature which gives you a quick way of finding particular information in a field. When it's turned on, each column heading has an arrow on the right hand side which can be used to apply a filter to the information in the column. You can apply filters to as many columns as you like and once a filter is applied to a column, the column title turns blue.

As well as specific filters you can apply interactive filters which display a dialog box during the filtering process. You then provide the information to the dialog box to allow it to complete the filtering process.

If none of the pre-defined filters meet your requirements you can create a custom filter that exactly matches your needs. You can copy an existing filter and then edit it to meet your needs or you can create a completely new filter. The Filter Definition dialog box has an entry bar to provide short cuts to simplify the process.

AutoFilter

When AutoFilter is turned on you can apply filters to any column. Use the All filter to remove any filter criteria and use the Custom filter to filter a column by more than one criterion.

1 Open your project in Task Sheet view.

2 Select View > Table > Usage from the Menu Bar. The relevant columns are displayed.

You can save an AutoFilter as a Custom filter for future reuse.

3 Click the AutoFilter button on the Toolbar. Down arrows appear on column headings.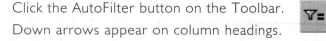

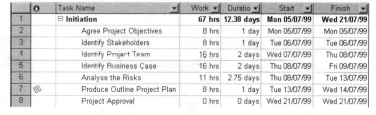

	❶	Task Name	Work ▼	Duratio ▼	Start ▼	Finish ▼
1		☐ Initiation	67 hrs	12.38 days	Mon 05/07/99	Wed 21/07/99
2		Agree Project Objectives	8 hrs	1 day	Mon 05/07/99	Mon 05/07/99
3		Identify Stakeholders	8 hrs	1 day	Tue 06/07/99	Tue 06/07/99
4		Identify Project Team	16 hrs	2 days	Wed 07/07/99	Thu 08/07/99
5		Identify Business Case	16 hrs	2 days	Thu 08/07/99	Fri 09/07/99
6		Analyse the Risks	11 hrs	2.75 days	Thu 08/07/99	Tue 13/07/99
7	✎	Produce Outline Project Plan	8 hrs	1 day	Tue 13/07/99	Wed 14/07/99
8		Project Approval	0 hrs	0 days	Wed 21/07/99	Wed 21/07/99

4 Click the 'Show All Subtasks' button on the Toolbar then click the Duration down arrow and select '> I day' (greater than I day). The view changes to only display tasks greater than I day's duration and the column heading is in blue.

5 Click the Duration down arrow and click 'All'. All tasks are displayed again.

6 Click the Work down arrow and select 'Custom'. Select Work 'is greater than or equal to' and type 12h. Click OK. The display is filtered accordingly.

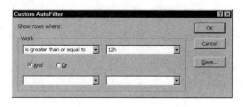

7 Click the AutoFilter button on the Toolbar again to turn it off. All tasks are displayed again.

Filter Criteria

You can specify filter criteria interactively if you often want to make a similar enquiry but with slightly different parameters. This is preferable to creating a large number of custom filters.

For example, you might want to get details of all tasks during the summer to check for any holiday implications.

1 Open your project in Task Sheet view and select View > Table > Schedule from the Menu Bar.

2 Select Project > Filtered for > Date Range from the Menu Bar. The Date Range dialog box opens.

3 Type 01/08/99 and click OK. The Date Range dialog box opens again for the end date.

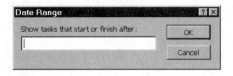

4 Type 31/08/99 and click OK. Only tasks that are due to be in progress in August are listed.

	Task Name	Start	Finish	Late Start	Late Finish
9	⊟ **Strategy**	**Wed 21/07/99**	**Mon 09/08/99**	**Mon 19/07/99**	**Tue 05/10/99**
15	Consolidate Res	Fri 30/07/99	Mon 02/08/99	Thu 29/07/99	Thu 29/07/99
16	Finalise Requirel	Mon 02/08/99	Tue 03/08/99	Fri 30/07/99	Fri 30/07/99
17	Evolve Other Rec	Tue 03/08/99	Wed 04/08/99	Mon 02/08/99	Mon 02/08/99
18	Carry Out Risk A	Wed 04/08/99	Fri 06/08/99	Tue 03/08/99	Wed 04/08/99
19	Produce Forwarc	Fri 06/08/99	Mon 09/08/99	Thu 05/08/99	Thu 05/08/99
20	Report to Manag	Fri 06/08/99	Mon 09/08/99	Fri 06/08/99	Mon 09/08/99
21	⊟ **Analysis**	**Tue 10/08/99**	**Tue 31/08/99**	**Tue 05/10/99**	**Tue 26/10/99**
22	Agree Requireml	Tue 10/08/99	Mon 16/08/99	Tue 05/10/99	Tue 12/10/99
23	Select Package	Tue 17/08/99	Mon 23/08/99	Tue 12/10/99	Tue 19/10/99
24	Purchase packa	Tue 24/08/99	Wed 25/08/99	Tue 19/10/99	Thu 21/10/99
25	Contingency	Thu 26/08/99	Tue 31/08/99	Thu 21/10/99	Tue 26/10/99

5 Click the Filter down arrow on the Toolbar and select All Tasks. All tasks are again displayed.

Filter by Resource

You can use resource filters to display tasks assigned to a resource. You can also use resource filters to change the resource information for one or more resources.

If the Facilities Group was going to change its name to Premises and you wanted to change all resources, you could use the resource filter to filter by that group name and then change it for all resources in the group.

1 Open your project in Resource Sheet view.

2 Click the Filter down arrow on the Toolbar and select Group... (notice the three dots which indicate further choices). The Group dialog box opens.

3 Type in 'Facilities' and click OK.
Now only the four Facilities resources are displayed.

4 Click the Resource Name column heading to select all resources. Then click the Resource Information button on the Toolbar. The Multiple Resource dialog box opens.

5 On the General tab, click in the Group field, type "Premises" and click OK. All resources have their Group changed to Premises.

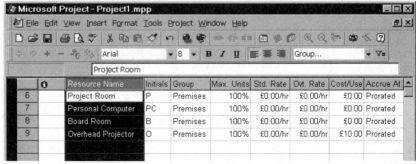

Custom Filters

Custom filters can be created from new or they can be created from an existing filter. The easiest way is to make a copy of an existing filter and then edit it.

The Filter Definition dialog box is used to name the filter, select the settings and define the criteria. A filter can have a single criterion or multiple criteria. Where multiple criteria are used they have to be separated by operators such as 'And' and 'Or' (And means both criteria must be met, Or means either or both can be met).

1   Open your project in Gantt Chart view and select Project > Filtered For > More Filters. The More Filters dialog box opens (this lists all filters).

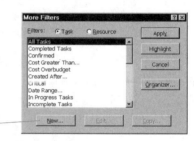

HANDY TIP

To copy an existing filter click Copy on the More Filters dialog box.

2   Click New. The Filter Definition dialog box opens.

3   Type the name "Start after 1 Sept".

4   Click in the first row under Field Name, click the down arrow and select 'Start'.

5   Click in the Test column, click the down arrow and select 'is greater than or equal to'.

6   Click in the Value(s) column and type "01/09/99" and click OK. The new filter is shown in the More Views dialog box.

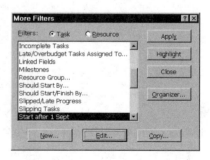

7   Click Apply and only the tasks from September are displayed.

Sorting

Tasks and resources are usually displayed in ascending ID Number order. However, you can sort by any field or even combination of fields by specifying sort keys.

1 Open your project in Task Sheet view and show all subtasks.

2 Select View > Table > Usage from the Menu Bar.

3 Select Project > Sort > Sort By from the Menu Bar. The Sort By dialog box opens.

4 Click the 'Sort by' down arrow, select 'Summary' and select the 'Descending' option. Click the 'Then by' down arrow, select 'Actual Duration' and select the 'Descending' option. Deselect 'Keep outline structure' and click Sort. The summary tasks are sorted first in descending sequence followed by the sub tasks in descending sequence.

REMEMBER

Combining sorting with filters gives you a powerful range of options.

	❶	Task Name	Work	Duration	Start	Finish
31		⊟ Implement	160 hrs	59.5 days	Wed 27/10/99	Fri 21/01/00
28		⊟ Build	240 hrs	30 days	Wed 15/09/99	Tue 26/10/99
21		⊟ Analysis	120 hrs	15 days	Tue 10/08/99	Tue 31/08/99
9		⊟ Strategy	128 hrs	13.63 days	Wed 21/07/99	Mon 09/08/99
1		⊟ Initiation	67 hrs	12.38 days	Mon 05/07/99	Wed 21/07/99
26		⊟ Design	80 hrs	10 days	Wed 01/09/99	Tue 14/09/99
10		⊟ Carry out Interviews	32 hrs	5 days	Wed 21/07/99	Wed 28/07/99
30		Contingency	200 hrs	25 days	Wed 22/09/99	Tue 26/10/99
27		Contingency	80 hrs	10 days	Wed 01/09/99	Tue 14/09/99
34		Contingency	80 hrs	10 days	Mon 10/01/00	Fri 21/01/00
22		Agree Requirements	40 hrs	5 days	Tue 10/08/99	Mon 16/08/99
23		Select Package	40 hrs	5 days	Tue 17/08/99	Mon 23/08/99
29		Install Package	40 hrs	5 days	Wed 15/09/99	Tue 21/09/99
32		Train Users	40 hrs	5 days	Wed 27/10/99	Tue 02/11/99
33	▥	Convert to New Package	40 hrs	5 days	Mon 03/01/00	Fri 07/01/00

Highlight Filters

When tasks and resources are filtered those that do not meet the criteria are hidden from view. Highlight filters can be used so that all tasks or resources are still visible but the tasks or resources that meet the criteria are highlighted in blue.

1   Open your project in Gantt Chart view and show all sub-tasks.

2   Select Project > Filter For > More Filters.

3   In the More Filters dialog box select 'Resource Group...' and click Highlight.

4   In the Resource Group dialog box type "Director" and click OK. The tasks with using a resource with the group Director, Bill Buggs (4, 5, 16 and 17) are highlighted in blue.

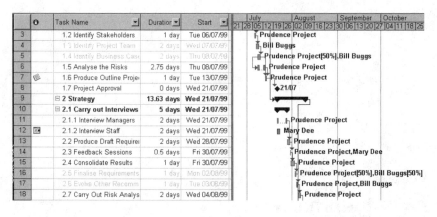

5   Click the Filter down arrow on the Toolbar and select 'All Tasks'.

The display returns to normal.

Tracking Progress

This chapter introduces progress tracking and entering progress information. It explains the different types of progress information and how to deal with them.

Chapter Twelve

Covers

Progress Tracking

Up to now you have been planning your project, allocating resources to it and then scheduling when things will happen. Once the project is actually under way you need to start tracking progress against your plan and schedule.

You enter information about your progress by using actual start and completion dates as well as effort expended by resource.

If tasks are completed ahead of schedule you can then decide if you want to bring other tasks forward. If tasks are running late you can decide what actions you can take to help.

Again, the Gantt chart is the most effective way of tracking progress as it can show actual against the plan.

Before you begin to enter actual information you should complete your plan in as much detail as you are able, using contingency figures where you do not have enough information. Once you are happy with the plan you should set a baseline (as described on page 113) and then start progress tracking.

Microsoft Project stores information under three headings:

Baseline   the plan dates which are compared with the actual and scheduled dates.

Actual   completed tasks or part-completed tasks.

Schedule   tasks that have not yet been started or work remaining on part-completed tasks.

The frequency with which you enter your information is up to you, but typically you would get progress details from the people working on the project at the end of each week.

As you enter your actual data the project is recalculated and rescheduled. So start at the earliest tasks on the schedule and work through. Once you have input all the actual information and seen the impact on the schedule you can re-evaluate the project and make any adjustments required to the project tasks to deal with issues that have arisen.

Progress Information

In addition to actual start and finish dates you can also input progress information on the percentage completed, actual and remaining duration, actual and remaining work and actual and remaining cost.

Depending on the type of information you input, Microsoft Project will calculate the other relevant information.

If you input a task completion date, Microsoft Project will set the actual start date to the scheduled start date and the actual duration to the difference between the start date and actual completion date.

The most accurate way of recording progress is to input the actual work done. This should be recorded by all the people resources you have working on the project. If this is less than the estimate for the task, Microsoft Project will then calculate the work remaining as the difference between the actual work done and the original estimate.

While Microsoft Project's calculation of the work to completion may be acceptable at the beginning of a task, it is far more accurate to get people to record their own estimates of the work required to complete their tasks at the same time as they record the work done. You can then input this information and get a picture of the way the project is really going.

You can also input actual duration and, if that is less than the scheduled duration, Microsoft Project calculates the remaining duration as the difference. If the task is actually completed in less than the scheduled duration, you need to set the remaining duration to zero. If it is going to be completed in less or more time you can again input your expected duration to completion.

In the same way, you can enter actual and remaining costs.

You can input task progress information in a number of views including Gantt Chart, Task Usage and Resource Usage views.

Completed Work

One a task has been completed, the easiest way to enter that information is simply by telling Microsoft Project that the task is completed.

1 Open your project in Gantt Chart view and select task 2 (Agree Project Objectives).

2 Select Tools > Tracking > Update Tasks from the menu Bar. The Update Tasks dialog box appears.

3 Click the Finish date down arrow, select the scheduled finish date (05/07/1999) and click OK.

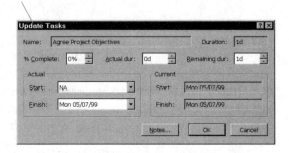

The task is now completed and a tick is displayed in the indicators field. The task is also removed from the critical path (it reverts to blue) and a progress bar (black line) is displayed through the task.

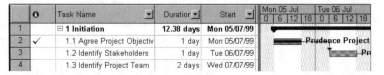

4 Select Tools > Tracking > Update Tasks from the Menu Bar again. The actual start and finish dates are entered, the task is shown as 100% complete, the actual duration is shown as 1 day and the remaining duration is set to zero.

5 Click Cancel. Position the cursor over the task indicator field. The date completed information pops up.

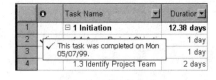

Part Completed Work

Where a number of hours or days of work have been carried out on a task but the task is not yet fully completed, you can enter the actual work carried out.

1 Open your project in Task Usage view and select task 3 (Identify Stakeholders).

2 Select Format > Details > Actual Work from the Menu Bar. The Actual Work fields are displayed underneath the estimated Work fields.

Click the Go To Selected Task button, if necessary, to bring the selected task into view.

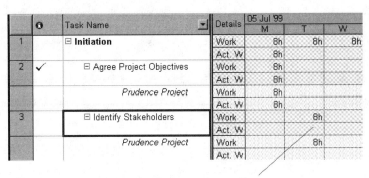

3 Click in the actual work field for the task.

4 Type 5 and press Enter.

		Task Name		Details	05 Jul 99		
					M	T	W
1		⊟ **Initiation**		Work	8h	5h	8h
				Act. W	8h	5h	
2	✓	⊟ Agree Project Objectives		Work	8h		
				Act. W	8h		
		Prudence Project		Work	8h		
				Act. W	8h		
3		⊟ Identify Stakeholders		Work		5h	3h
				Act. W		5h	
		Prudence Project		Work		5h	3h
				Act. W		5h	

The actual hours are entered, the work is rescheduled from 8 to 5 hours and the remaining 3 hours are rescheduled for the following day.

Percentage Completed

There is a certain amount of risk involved in using percentage completed as the measure of work done on a task. It is human nature for most people to be optimistic about their progress so a measure of actual work done and estimate of work to completion is usually more accurate. However, it will sometimes be appropriate to use percentage completed where it's not practical to track work more closely.

1 Open your project in Task Sheet view.

2 Select View > More Views > Task Sheet from the Menu Bar and click Apply.

3 Select View > Table > Tracking from the Menu Bar.

4 Select View > Toolbars > Tracking from the Menu Bar.

5 Select task 4 (Identify Project Team) and click the 75% Complete button on the Tracking Toolbar.

	Task Name	Act. Star	Act. Finis	% Com	Act. Du	Rem. Du	Act. Cos	Act. Wo
1	⊟ Initiation	Mon 05/07/99	NA	35%	4.41 days	8.34 days	£740.00	25 hrs
2	Agree Project Objectives	Mon 05/07/99	Mon 05/07/99	100%	1 day	0 days	£160.00	8 hrs
3	Identify Stakeholders	Tue 06/07/99	NA	73%	1 day	0.38 days	£100.00	5 hrs
4	Identify Project Team	Wed 07/07/99	NA	75%	1.5 days	0.5 days	£480.00	12 hrs
5	Identify Business Case	NA	NA	0%	0 days	2 days	£0.00	0 hrs

You can input and adjust any percentage figure using the Update Tasks dialog box.

The Actual Start date is entered as scheduled. The percentage completed is set to 75% and the Actual Duration, Remaining Duration, Actual Cost and Actual Work fields are all updated.

6 Select View > Gantt Chart from the Menu Bar. The part completed tasks are shown with progress bars.

	ⓘ	Task Name	Duration	Start	05 Jul 99 S M T W T F S
1		⊟ 1 Initiation	12.75 days	Mon 05/07/99	
2	✓	1.1 Agree Project Objectiv	1 day	Mon 05/07/99	Prudence Proj
3		1.2 Identify Stakeholders	1.38 days	Tue 06/07/99	Prudence
4		1.3 Identify Project Team	2 days	Wed 07/07/99	Bill
5		1.4 Identify Business Case	2 days	Thu 08/07/99	

Duration Completed

In the same way as you can enter actual work done, you can also enter actual and remaining duration for a task.

1   Open your project in Gantt Chart view and select task 5 (Identify Business Case).

2   Select Tools > Tracking > Update Tasks from the Menu bar. The Update Tasks dialog box opens.

If you have the Tracking Toolbar displayed you can click the Update Tasks button.

3   Click the Actual Duration up arrow to display 1 day then click OK.

If you get a task scheduling conflict warning select 'Ignore'.

The task is updated on the Gantt Chart.

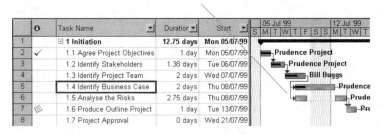

4   Select Tools > Tracking > Update Tasks again from the Menu bar.

Note that the Percentage completed is set to 50%, the Actual and Remaining duration are set to 1 day and the Actual start date is set to the scheduled start date.

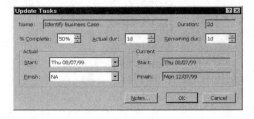

Click Cancel and save your project file.

Entering Costs

Normally Microsoft Project calculates actual costs for you based on the actual work and the cost details you have entered for the resource. However, you can also enter actual cost details directly.

1 Select Tools > Options from the Menu bar. The Options dialog box opens.

2 Click the Calculation tab.

3 Clear the 'Actual costs are always calculated by Microsoft Project' check box and click OK.

4 Select View > Task Usage from the Menu bar.

5 Select View > Table > Tracking from the Menu bar.

6 Select Format > Details > Actual Cost from the Menu bar.

You can only enter actual costs for completed tasks.

7 Click in task 2, Actual Cost field, type 200 and press Enter.

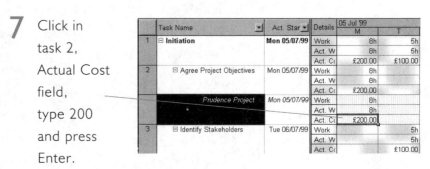

8 Close your file without saving.

Updating as Scheduled

One or more tasks that have been started and/or completed as scheduled can be updated using the Update As Scheduled button on the Tracking Toolbar or the Update Project dialog box.

1 Open your project in Gantt Chart view.

2 Select Tools > Tracking > Update Project to open the Update Project dialog box.

3 Select 'Update work as completed through', set the date to 12/07/1999 and click OK.

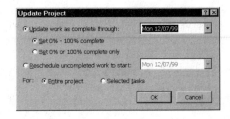

If you get a scheduling conflict warning select Continue and click OK. The tasks are now all shown as completed up to 12 July and task 6 (Analyse the Risks) is shown as part completed up to 12 July.

4 Select task 6 (Analyse the Risks) and click the Update Tasks button on the Tracking Toolbar.

The task is shown at 73% completed with 2 days actual and 0.75 days remaining.
Click Cancel.

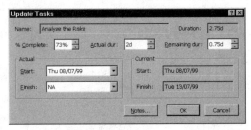

Actual v Baseline

Having set the project baseline you can monitor your actual progress against the baseline at any time. The baseline and actual figures can be displayed in a number of Tables, through the use of Filters and in the Tracking Gantt Chart view.

Table Views

1. In Gantt Chart view select task 6 (Analyse the Risks) and click the Update Tasks button on the Tracking Toolbar.

You can use the up and down arrows to step one day at a time.

2. Increase the Actual duration to 4 days, the Remaining duration to 1 day and click OK. You will

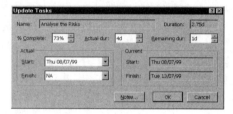

receive a warning that you have gone outside the original duration for the task. Click OK and the project will be rescheduled.

3. Select View > Table > Work from the Menu bar and the Work Table view opens.(Note that Work represents Actual + Remaining and Variance is the difference between Work and Baseline.)

Use the Filter down arrow on the Toolbar to display Over budget or Slipping tasks.

	Task Name	Work	Baseline	Variance	Actual	Remaining
1	⊟ 1 Initiation	71.5 hrs	67 hrs	4.5 hrs	61.5 hrs	10 hrs
2	1.1 Agree Project Objectives	8 hrs	8 hrs	0 hrs	8 hrs	0 hrs
3	1.2 Identify Stakeholders	8 hrs	8 hrs	0 hrs	8 hrs	0 hrs
4	1.3 Identify Project Team	16 hrs	16 hrs	0 hrs	16 hrs	0 hrs
5	1.4 Identify Business Case	16 hrs	16 hrs	0 hrs	16 hrs	0 hrs
6	1.5 Analyse the Risks	15.5 hrs	11 hrs	4.5 hrs	13.5 hrs	2 hrs

4. Select View > Table > Cost to see the Actual and Baseline cost, and View > Table > Variance to see the start and finish date variance from Baseline.

Tracking Gantt Chart

The Tracking Gantt Chart gives you a graphical representation of the actual state of the project compared to the baseline.

1 Select View > Tracking Gantt from the Menu bar and adjust your view so that it looks like the following:

	O	Task Name	Duration	Start	05 Jul 99 / 12 Jul 99 / 19 Jul 99
1		⊟ Initiation	15 days	Mon 05/07/99	84%
2	✓	Agree Project Objective	1 day	Mon 05/07/99	100%
3	✓	Identify Stakeholders	1.38 days	Tue 06/07/99	100%
4	✓	Identify Project Team	2 days	Wed 07/07/99	100%
5	✓	Identify Business Case	2 days	Thu 08/07/99	100%
6		Analyse the Risks	5 days	Thu 08/07/99	80%
7		Produce Outline Project	1 day	Fri 16/07/99	0%
8		Project Approval	0 days	Fri 23/07/99	◇ 23/07

Note the following:

- Actual progress is shown as a hatched line underneath summary task 1 (Initiation).
- The baseline is shown in grey beneath the actual and scheduled task bars.
- For task 2 (Agree Project Objectives) the actual and baseline are the same as the task was completed to schedule.
- Task 3 (Identify Stakeholders) started on schedule but was completed 0.38 days late.
- Tasks 4 and 5 were completed to the estimated duration (2 days each) but were started late (due to task 3) and therefore finished late.
- Task 6 started late and will be completed even later so task 7 will also start and finish late.
- Finally, the baseline milestone (an empty diamond) shows that the scheduled milestone (a solid diamond) will be 2 days late.

HANDY TIP **Having some lag time in your schedule allows you to cope with task delays without throwing out the whole schedule.**

2 Click on the dependency line from task 7 to task 8 and reduce the lag from 5 to 3 days. This will bring the project back on schedule.

Project Statistics

The Project Statistics dialog box gives you summary level information for the whole project.

1 Select Project > Project Information from the Menu bar.
The Project Information dialog box opens.

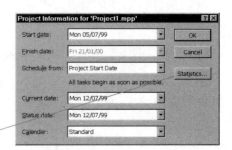

2 Click Statistics. The Project Statistics dialog box opens.

You can also click the Project Statistics button on the Tracking Toolbar. It looks like this:

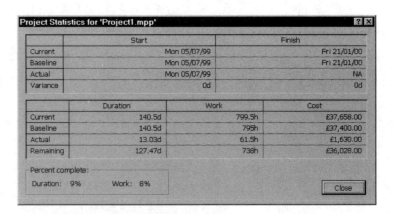

The top section shows the current, baseline, actual and variance for the start and finish dates.

The middle section shows statistics on the duration, work and cost of the project.

Note that despite some of the tasks in stage 1 (Initiation) running late we have kept the project on schedule by reducing the lag time. However, we are currently over budget on the Work and Cost.

The final section shows the overall percentage completed in Duration and Work.

Progress Lines

Progress Lines can be drawn on the Gantt Chart or Tracking Gantt Chart at any date to show the actual or expected progress at that date.

They work by linking the tasks that are scheduled to be started, completed or in progress on that date. Tasks that are behind schedule result in peaks to the left of the line, and tasks that are ahead of schedule result in peaks to the right of the line.

I Open your project in Gantt Chart view and make sure the Tracking Toolbar is displayed.

2 Click the Add Progress Line button on the Tracking Toolbar.
The cursor changes to a jagged line with an arrow either side.

3 Move the cursor over the Gantt Chart until the pop-up box displays a Progress Date of 16 July.

Progress Line	
Progress Date:	Fri 16/07/99
Click the mouse to display a progress line on this date	

4 Click on that date and the progress line will be displayed on the chart.

	o	Task Name	Duration	Start	05 Jul 99 / 12 Jul 99
1		⊟ **Initiation**	**13 days**	**Mon 05/07/99**	
2	✓	Agree Project Objective	1 day	Mon 05/07/99	100%
3	✓	Identify Stakeholders	1.38 days	Tue 06/07/99	100%
4	✓	Identify Project Team	2 days	Wed 07/07/99	100%
5	✓	Identify Business Case	2 days	Thu 08/07/99	100%
6		Analyse the Risks	5 days	Thu 08/07/99	80%
7	✎	Produce Outline Project	1 day	Fri 16/07/99	0%
8		Project Approval	0 days	Wed 21/07/99	

5 To remove a progress line, double-click the line and the Progress Lines dialog box opens. Click Delete then click OK and the progress line is removed.

HANDY TIP

You can place multiple progress lines on a chart and delete any of them in the Progress Lines dialog box.

When is a Task Completed?

This chapter has concentrated on tracking progress of your project by entering details of tasks and work completed. But one of the difficult decisions facing a project manager is exactly when do you treat a task as completed?

The old quotation used to be "The job's not over until the paperwork's done." Usually accompanied by a picture of a small child on a potty!

The more formal answer is that the task has been completed when everything that needs to be done has been done. If the task was to produce something tangible like a report or specification then the task is not completed until the product has been produced and formally signed off. This should include any quality control or management approval.

Experienced project managers will be aware of the 80% completed syndrome. This is a reflection of peoples' basic optimism when estimating the work remaining to complete a task. This is the reason why using percentage completed figures is not usually very accurate.

So to be realistic, use the actual work effort used and the estimated work to completion. In the early stages of a task these should add up to the work estimated for the task. As the task progresses they should begin to show if the task is going to take more or less work than the estimate. And there should be no sudden last minute surprises.

REMEMBER

The job's not over until the paperwork's done!

If someone is estimating that they will be completing a task to estimate until the very last moment and then it suddenly increases, they were not being realistic. As the project manager you should feed that back to them (in a constructive way) so that they will hopefully be more accurate in future tasks.

Finally, if they have used up all the estimated time and the task is still not formally completed or signed off then they should still be showing some work to completion.

Customising

This chapter introduces the customising of tables, views and reports in Microsoft Project. It also shows you how to share customised items between projects.

Chapter Thirteen

Customising Microsoft Project

Microsoft Project has a large number of pre-defined tables, views and report formats. These will probably cover most requirements for most projects. However, if you do need a different table, view or report format, Microsoft Project allows you to customise or create new ones.

In addition to being able to change the sequence of columns in a table, view or report, there are over 200 different fields holding information that you can access and use in Microsoft Project. With this amount of information available you should be able to create exactly what you require for your project.

Tables

Tables are made up of columns and rows of information and there are 27 pre-defined task and resource tables available in Microsoft Project. If none of these match your requirements you can create your own custom tables to include exactly the information you require. You can also combine your custom tables with pre-defined or custom filters (described in chapter 11).

Views

Microsoft Project contains 26 pre-defined views which display schedule information and allow you to edit it. Some of these views are single views and some are combination views. Single views consist of a screen, table and filter. Combination views combine two single views on the same screen by splitting them one above the other. Custom views can be built based on any combination.

Reports

Microsoft Project contains 25 pre-defined reports split into five report groups. Custom reports can be based on any of these existing reports or they can be created completely from new. If you create a new report it can be based on one of four report templates: task report, resource report, monthly calendar report and crosstab report.

Custom Tables

Custom tables can be created from new but it is usually easier to copy an existing table and then edit it.

1 Open your project in Gantt Chart view, select View > Table > More Tables > Summary from the Menu bar, then click Copy. The Table Definition dialog box opens with a copy of the Summary table displayed.

2 Type 'Project Summary Table' in the Name.

3 In the Field Name column select Duration and click Delete Row. The row is deleted from the definitions. Now delete Finish and Cost in the same way.

4 Now select %Complete and click Insert Row. Click the down arrow, select Actual Start and press Tab. The default values are inserted for the other fields. Now insert Actual Work in front of %Complete.

You can also press Enter or select another field to insert the default values.

5 Select Work and click Cut Row. Select Actual Work and click Paste Row.

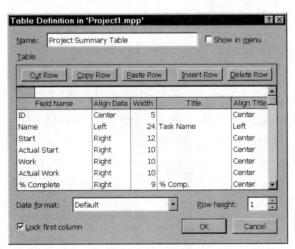

Table Definition in 'Project1.mpp'

Name: Project Summary Table   ☐ Show in menu

Table

| Cut Row | Copy Row | Paste Row | Insert Row | Delete Row |

Field Name	Align Data	Width	Title	Align Title
ID	Center	5		Center
Name	Left	24	Task Name	Left
Start	Right	12		Center
Actual Start	Right	10		Center
Work	Right	10		Center
Actual Work	Right	10		Center
% Complete	Right	9	% Comp.	Center

Date format: Default   Row height: 1

☑ Lock first column   OK   Cancel

6 Click OK and then click Apply. The new table is applied to your Gantt Chart view.

Custom Views

Custom views can be created as single views or as combination views. First we will create a new single view.

1. Open your project, select View > More Views from the Menu bar and click New.
   The Define New View dialog box opens.

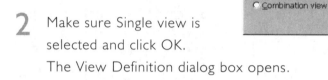

2. Make sure Single view is selected and click OK.
   The View Definition dialog box opens.

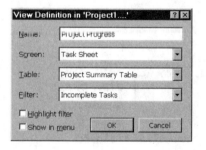

3. Type the name 'Project Progress', select 'Task Sheet', 'Project Summary Table', 'Incomplete Tasks' and click OK. The More Views box is displayed again.

4. Make sure that 'Project Progress' is selected and click Apply. The new Project Progress single view is displayed with all incomplete tasks (tasks that are in progress or not yet started) displayed:

	Task Name	Start	Actual Start	Work	Actual Work	% Comp.
1	⊟ Initiation	Mon 05/07/99	Mon 05/07/99	71.5 hrs	61.5 hrs	84%
6	Analyse the Risks	Thu 08/07/99	Thu 08/07/99	15.5 hrs	13.5 hrs	80%
7	Produce Outline Proj	Fri 16/07/99	NA	8 hrs	0 hrs	0%
8	Project Approval	Wed 21/07/99	NA	0 hrs	0 hrs	0%
9	⊟ Strategy	Thu 22/07/99	NA	128 hrs	0 hrs	0%
10	⊟ Carry out Interviews	Thu 22/07/99	NA	32 hrs	0 hrs	0%
11	Interview Manage	Thu 22/07/99	NA	16 hrs	0 hrs	0%
12	Interview Staff	Thu 22/07/99	NA	16 hrs	0 hrs	0%
13	Produce Draft Require	Thu 29/07/99	NA	16 hrs	0 hrs	0%
14	Feedback Sessions	Mon 02/08/99	NA	8 hrs	0 hrs	0%
15	Consolidate Results	Mon 02/08/99	NA	8 hrs	0 hrs	0%
16	Finalise Requirement	Tue 03/08/99	NA	8 hrs	0 hrs	0%
17	Evolve Other Recomn	Wed 04/08/99	NA	16 hrs	0 hrs	0%
18	Carry Out Risk Analy	Thu 19/08/99	NA	16 hrs	0 hrs	0%
19	Produce Forward Pla	Mon 23/08/99	NA	8 hrs	0 hrs	0%
20	Report to Managemer	Fri 06/08/99	NA	16 hrs	0 hrs	0%

Combination View

To create a combination view we can use our new custom view and combine it with another view.

1 Select View > More Views from the Menu bar and click New.

2 Select Combination view and click OK.

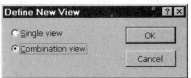

3 Type the name 'Progress Review', select 'Detail Gantt' for the Top and 'Project Progress' for the Bottom, click OK and then click Apply in More Views. The new combination view is displayed.

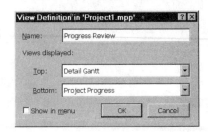

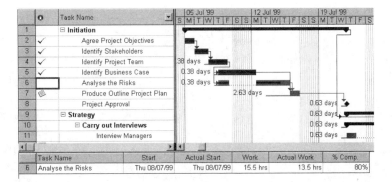

4 Move up and down the tasks in the top pane and the relevant task progress details are displayed in the bottom pane.

5 To display details of several tasks in the bottom pane select multiple tasks by dragging across them in the top pane.

Custom Reports

While you can always produce a custom report by starting with an existing report which is close to your requirements and then customising it, you may sometimes want to produce a completely new report.

1 Select View > Reports > Custom and click Select. The Custom Reports dialog box opens.

2 Select 'Project Summary' and note that the Copy button is not selectable.
Click New and the Define New Report dialog box opens.

3 Select 'Crosstab' and click OK.
The Crosstab Report definition box opens.

4 Type the name 'Weekly Project Costs', select Row: 'Tasks' and 'Cost'.
On the Details tab select Show Column totals and click OK. The Custom Reports dialog box is displayed.

5 Select 'Weekly Project Costs' and click Preview.
Your report should look something like the following:

Weekly Project Costs as of Mon 05/07/99
Financial System Upgrade
Your Name

	05/07	12/07	19/07	26/07	02/08	09/08
Agree Project Objectives	£160.00					
Identify Stakeholders	£160.00					
Identify Project Team	£640.00					
Identify Business Case	£280.00	£120.00				
Analyse the Risks	£66.00	£244.00				
Produce Outline Project Plan		£160.00				
Project Approval						
Interview Managers			£160.00	£160.00		
Interview Staff			£240.00			
Produce Draft Requirements				£320.00		
Feedback Sessions					£140.00	
Consolidate Results					£160.00	
Finalise Requirements					£240.00	
Evolve Other Recommendations					£480.00	
Carry Out Risk Analysis						
Produce Forward Plan						
Report to Management					£160.00	£160.00
Total	£1,306.00	£524.00	£400.00	£480.00	£1,180.00	£160.00

Sharing Custom Items

Any custom tables, views or reports that you create in Microsoft Project are stored in the project file you created them in. However, you can make these items available to other projects by using the Organizer.

I   Open your project file and click the New button on the Toolbar. A new blank project is created and the Project Information dialog box opens.

2   Click Cancel, then select File > Save As from the Menu bar and save the file as 'Share Test'.

3   Select View > Table > More Tables from the Menu bar and click Organizer. The Organizer dialog box opens at the Tables tab.

4   In the bottom left hand corner (Tables available in) select your project.

5   Select 'Project Summary Table' and click Copy.
The project Summary Table is copied to the new project file.

6   Click Close and the More Tables dialog box is displayed.

7   Select 'Project Summary Table' and click Apply.
The Project Summary Table is applied to the view.

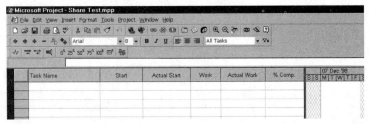

A Word of Caution

Although Microsoft Project allows you to customise and change just about every table, view and report, it is good practice to use a copy of a pre-defined item and not change the pre-defined items themselves.

That way if you make a mistake you can just delete the new item and start again.

Murphy has a word of caution as well:

Murphy's 2nd Law

Anything you try and change will take much longer and cost much more than you thought

Murphy's Second Law applies to just about everything and projects in particular. If your project involves computers or channel tunnels it is widely believed that the impact of Murphy's Second Law doubles!

On the subject of Murphy, here's another relevant one:

Murphy's 3rd Law

If everything seems to be going well, you obviously don't know what's going on

Hyperlinks and HTML

This chapter explains hyperlinks and how to create them. It goes on to cover the creation of HTML and GIF files for publishing on the Web, and finally creating an export map.

Covers

Chapter Fourteen

Using Hyperlinks

Hyperlinks were developed on the World Wide Web and provide a simple way of jumping from inside one document to another document. With a hyperlink you can not only jump to another document on your own computer or on your local area network, but you can jump to another document anywhere on the Web (assuming you have an Internet connection).

With a hyperlink you can even open the document you are linking to at any particular point in that document that has a reference.

To follow a hyperlink you just click on it. Pausing your cursor over a hyperlink will usually display some information about it, such as its address in the form of a Uniform Resource Locator (URL) – ie:

http://www.computerstep.com

In Microsoft Project you can create a hyperlink to another document on any task, resource or assignment using the Insert Hyperlink button.

The hyperlink symbol is displayed in the Indicators field and the hyperlink details are stored in the Hyperlink field. You can also insert a hyperlink in a text column on a sheet view.

Documents published on the World Wide Web are written in a language called HyperText Markup Language (HTML) which is read and interpreted by a program called a Web Browser. Microsoft Internet Explorer is one of the most widely used web browsers. If you have a web browser on your computer, clicking on a hypertext link to a HTML document in Microsoft Project will open your browser and then open the HTML document in it. Closing it will return you to Microsoft Project.

If the hypertext link is to a Word or Excel document on your computer or network, Microsoft Project will open Word or Excel and then open the document in that program. Closing it will return you to Microsoft Project.

Inserting a Hypertext Link

Adding a hypertext link to a project is very straight forward.

1 Create the following simple HTML file using a text editor
   (such as Windows Notepad):

```
<HTML>
<HEAD>
<TITLE>Simple HTML File</TITLE>
</HEAD>
<BODY>
A simple HTML file.
</BODY>
</HTML>
```

Save the file with a .htm extension.

2 Open your project in Gantt Chart view, select task 6
   (Analyse the Risks) and click the Insert Hyperlink button
   on the Toolbar.
   The Insert Hyperlink
   dialog box opens.

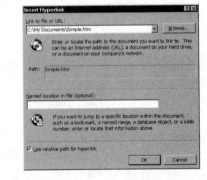

HANDY TIP

If you don't have a Web Browser, create a link to a Word document or other type of file.

3 Click Browse, locate your
   HTML file and click OK.
   The hypertext symbol is
   inserted in the Indicator
   field.

4 Pause your cursor over the hypertext symbol. The cursor
   changes to a pointing
   finger and the file name
   pops up.

5 Click on the link to jump to the file. Your browser opens and
   displays the file. Click Back (or close the browser) to return.

Publishing to HTML

Project data can be saved from Microsoft Project in HTML format for publishing as Web pages on the Internet or on an internal Intranet. While you cannot save the entire project as an HTML file, you can save data from it.

Data is saved using import/export maps which determine which fields of data will be exported.

1   Open your project and select File > Save As HTML from the Menu bar. The File Save dialog box opens.

2   Select the directory where you want to export the file to, type in a file name and click Save.
The Export Format dialog box opens.

3   Select 'Top Level Tasks list' and click Save.
The file is saved into your selected directory.

4   View the file in your Web Browser.

HANDY TIP
If you don't have a Web Browser, view the file in a text editor so you can see the HTML.

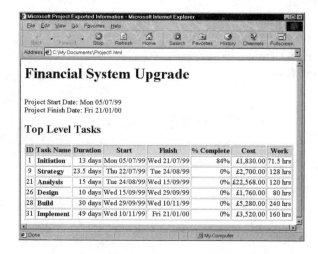

Financial System Upgrade

Project Start Date: Mon 05/07/99
Project Finish Date: Fri 21/01/00

Top Level Tasks

ID	Task Name	Duration	Start	Finish	% Complete	Cost	Work
1	Initiation	13 days	Mon 05/07/99	Wed 21/07/99	84%	£1,830.00	71.5 hrs
9	Strategy	23.5 days	Thu 22/07/99	Tue 24/08/99	0%	£2,700.00	128 hrs
21	Analysis	15 days	Tue 24/08/99	Wed 15/09/99	0%	£22,568.00	120 hrs
26	Design	10 days	Wed 15/09/99	Wed 29/09/99	0%	£1,760.00	80 hrs
28	Build	30 days	Wed 29/09/99	Wed 10/11/99	0%	£5,280.00	240 hrs
31	Implement	49 days	Wed 10/11/99	Fri 21/01/00	0%	£3,520.00	160 hrs

Copying to GIF Files

Although the export maps are useful and can be edited, you can only export data to HTML files. If you want to export a picture like a Gantt Chart you need to export it as a GIF (Graphic Image Format) file.

This is done through the Copy Picture facility.

1 Open your project in Gantt Chart view.

2 Click the Copy Picture button on the Toolbar. The Copy Picture dialog box opens.

3 Select 'Render image to GIF Image file', 'Copy Rows on screen', 'Timescale as shown on screen', and click OK.

4 Now view the GIF file using your web browser or other suitable utility.
It should look like the following:

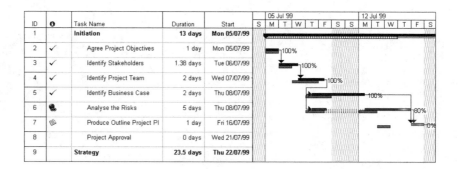

Once you have created a GIF file of the image you want to use, you can include it in an export map. This is covered in the next topic.

Export Maps

You could try out some of the other export maps such as 'Export to HTML using standard template' which lists the tasks, resources and assignments.

In addition to the pre-defined export maps you can also edit existing export maps or define new ones.

1. Select File > Save As HTML from the Menu bar and click Save. The Export Format dialog box opens.

2. Click New Map. The Define Import/Export Map dialog box opens.

3. Type the name 'Test Map', select 'Include image file in HTML page' and select the GIF file you created in the last topic.

4. Click Data to import/export Tasks. The Task Mapping tab becomes active, select it.

5. Click in the From project field and select ID, Name, Start, Work and Cost.
   Click OK.
   The Export Format dialog box is displayed.

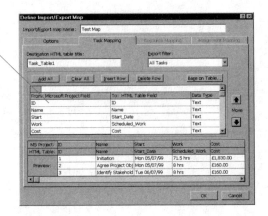

6. Select 'Test Map' and click Save.
   The HTML file is saved.

7. View the HTML file using your web browser.
   The Gantt Chart is displayed as a graphic image followed by your data in a table.

PERT Charts

This chapter explains what PERT Charts are and how to use them. It shows you how to add nodes, change dependencies and format the chart.

Chapter Fifteen

PERT Charts

PERT (Programme Evaluation and Review Techniques) Charts are also sometimes referred to as Activity Diagrams. They give you a graphical view of tasks and dependencies. Each task is shown as a box (called a node) which can display up to five fields. The default fields are task name, task ID, scheduled duration, scheduled start date and scheduled finish date. The lines linking the tasks reflect the task dependencies.

The border around each task denotes what level or type of task it is:

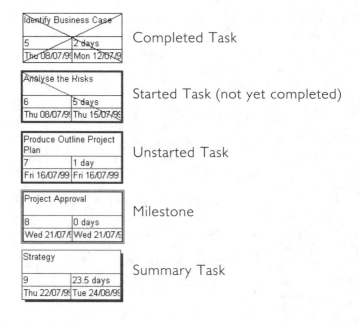

Tasks on the critical path are shown in red with a heavy border, tasks not on the critical path are shown in black with a thin border, milestones have a double border and summary tasks have a drop shadow.

The PERT Chart provides a different type of view of the project from the Gantt Chart but any changes made in either are reflected in the project and the other views.

PERT Chart View

Although PERT Charts are no longer as popular as they once were (having been largely replaced by the Gantt Chart) they still provide a useful alternate view of a project.

1   Open your project in Gantt Chart view and select task 6 (Analyse the Risks).

2   Select View > PERT Chart from the Menu bar. The PERT Chart is displayed centred on task 6 (which is selected).

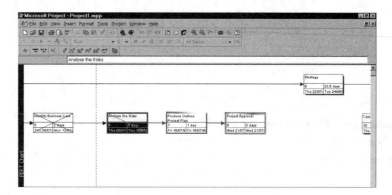

3   Use the Zoom In and Zoom Out buttons on the Toolbar together with the scroll bars to move around the PERT Chart. Note that if you try to zoom in to more than 400% or out to less than 25% you get a warning.

4   Find task 15 (Consolidate Results), select it by clicking on it and select View > Tracking Gantt from the Menu bar.
Note that task 15 is also selected in the Tracking Gantt.
Click on the Go To Selected Task button on the Toolbar to bring the task into view on the Gantt Chart.
Moving between PERT and Gantt views is very simple.

5   Switch back to PERT Chart view and double click on task 16 (Finalise Requirements). The Task Information dialog box opens so that you can make any changes.

Adding a Node

In addition to being able to amend task details in PERT Chart view, you can also add a new node (task) to the chart.

When you inserted a task in Gantt Chart view, it was inserted in front of the selected task. In PERT Chart view a new task is inserted after the selected task.

The F5 key is a short cut to Go To a Task.

1 Open your project in PERT Chart view and select task 22 (Agree Requirements) by pressing F5, type 22 and then Enter. Task 22 is selected and positioned in the view.

2 Below and to the right of task 22, drag the cursor to create a box (if you get a conflict warning choose Continue). A new task 26 is inserted with the name field selected.

Your box will be re-sized to the same size as the other nodes.

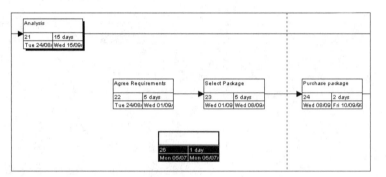

3 Type 'Issue Requirements' and press Enter. The duration is automatically set to the default of 1 day.

4 Select task 25 (Contingency), click in the Duration field, type 2 and press Enter. Contingency duration is reduced to 2 days.

5 Save your project file.

As you identify and add tasks to the later stages of a project you should reduce your contingency figure accordingly to keep the overall duration constant.

Changing Dependencies

Once you have added a new node or task you will normally need to make changes to the dependencies to incorporate it.

In PERT Chart view you select existing dependencies by double clicking on the linking lines. To create a new dependency you drag from the preceding task to the dependent task. By default a finish-to-start dependency is created. You can then double click on the line to make any changes.

1   Place your cursor on task 22 (Agree requirements) and drag down to task 26 (Issue Requirements).
    When you release the mouse button the dependency is created.

2   Now create a dependency from task 26 (Issue Requirements) to task 23 (Select Package).
    The dependency between task 22 and task 23 is now referred to as a redundant dependency (as it is implied by the new dependencies you have inserted).

3   Double click on the dependency line between task 22 and task 23.
    The Task Dependency pop-up box opens.

4   Click Delete.
    The redundant dependency is removed.

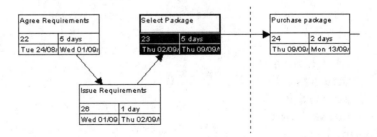

There are still a couple of things that need to be edited on this change.

Aligning Nodes

There are a number of things that you can change on the PERT Chart layout including aligning new nodes, changing the way nodes are linked and changing the information displayed in the nodes.

First let's align the node we inserted in the previous topic.

 If you have Viewbar selected you can switch between views with one mouse click.

1. Select task 26 and switch to Gantt Chart view.
   The new task has been inserted as a first level task.
   Click the Indent button on the Toolbar to indent it to the correct level.

2. Switch back to PERT Chart view and click the Zoom Out button on the Toolbar to reduce the scale to 25%.
   This will let you see what is going on (although you won't be able to read the task information!).

3. Select Format > Layout Now from the Menu bar.
   The view now displays the first task in the project.

 Use F5 to select a task.

4. Select task 26 and click the Zoom In button.
   The new task has been correctly aligned between task 22 and task 23.

One other thing you may wish to do is to renumber the tasks so they run sequentially.

 Make sure you have an arrow cursor (not a plus sign) before you drag.

5. Switch back to Gantt Chart view and select task 26 by clicking on the task ID.

6. Drag the task into position between task 22 and task 23.
   When you release the mouse button the tasks are renumbered.
   Switch back to PERT Chart view.

Changing Node Format

The box and border style options allow you to change the fields of information that are displayed, the format of the information displayed, and the layout and colour of the nodes.

1 Open your project in PERT Chart view and ensure you have some white space (an area of chart with no nodes in it) available.

2 Double click on a blank area of the chart. The Box Styles dialog box opens.

3 Select the Borders tab and then select the different Items to see the default way they are displayed. Click on the Style or Colour to make any changes.

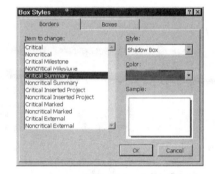

4 Select the Boxes tab, click on the down arrow beside field 2 (ID), select 'Outline Number' from the list and click OK.
The nodes now show the outline number in place of the task ID.

You can also change the date format (to include date and time if required) and the text size on the Boxes tab.

Changing the Layout

Finally you can also change the way that the connecting lines are displayed.

1   Select Format > Layout from the Menu bar.
     The Layout dialog box opens.

2   Select the second Links
     option and
     clear page breaks.

3   Click OK.
     The PERT Chart's layout is
     re-formatted.

4   Zoom out to view the chart.
     The connectors are now displayed with right-angles and the
     dotted lines (indicating the page breaks) have been
     removed.

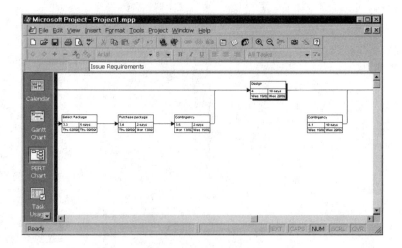

REMEMBER **To change
the boxes
back to
show ID's,
just double click on
a blank part of the
view.**

5   Change the layout back to show page breaks and save your
     project file.

Assigning Resources

You can also deal with assigning resources to a task in PERT Chart view in one of two ways. You can allocate a field in the node box to resource name or resource initials and then type it directly into the field. Alternatively, you can use the Task Information dialog box.

Although we created a new task 23 (Issue Requirements) in an earlier topic, we have not yet assigned a resource to it.

1 Press F5, type 23 and press Enter to select task 23 and bring it into view on the chart.

2 Double-click on task 23 (Issue Requirements). The Task Information dialog box opens.

3 Select the Resources tab and click in the Resource name field. Click the down arrow, select your project manager and click OK.

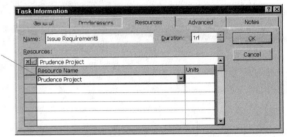

4 Switch back to Gantt Chart view and adjust the time scale to bring the relevant tasks into view.
The task has correctly been assigned to your project manager.

Task PERT Chart

There is a PA_PERT Entry Sheet – but it's a Gantt Chart view really!

In addition to the basic PERT Chart view there is also a Task PERT Chart. This shows the selected task with its predecessor and successor tasks and is useful in sorting out dependency problems.

By combining the PERT Chart and Task PERT Chart views you can explore the dependencies in some detail.

1 Open your project in PERT Chart view and select task 13 (Produce Draft Requirements).

2 Move your cursor to the bottom right-hand corner of the screen so that it changes into the split bar symbol.

3 Double-click while the split bar symbol is displayed. The screen splits and the Task Form view is displayed in the lower half of the screen.

4 Click in the lower pane to make it active.

5 Select View > More Views > Task PERT and click Apply. The Task PERT view is displayed in the lower pane.

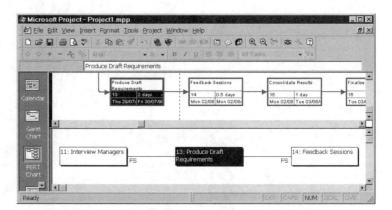

6 Click on different task nodes in the top pane. The dependencies are displayed in the lower pane.

Programme Management

This chapter explores the various multiple project environments and shows you how to consolidate projects, share resources and deal with inter-project dependencies.

Covers

Chapter Sixteen

Projects and Programmes

While a project may stand on its own, increasingly, as businesses develop strategic level plans, a project may be a part of a much larger and long term programme consisting of many projects.

In current programme management parlance a Programme may consist of a number of Tranches, which in turn consist of a number of Projects. These Projects are sometimes grouped together and referred to as a Project Portfolio.

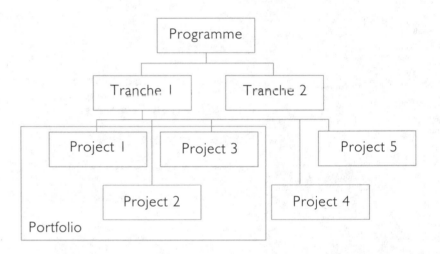

If your project is part of a portfolio, tranche or programme (or you are responsible for managing a portfolio, tranche or programme) your project will not exist in isolation.

Microsoft Project provides a way of working with multiple projects that allows you to bring all the projects together to see how they relate. You can work with the individual projects when you need to and then consolidate them together for the big picture.

It also allows you to allocate resources across multiple projects and keep control of them. You can set up one master set of resources and maintain them in one place while still using them on multiple projects. Then if changes occur to the resources, you only have to make them in one place.

Consolidating Projects

If you are responsible for more than one related project, whatever the grouping is called, you can create a consolidated project file to contain them and control them.

You consolidate projects by inserting them into the consolidated project file. Microsoft Project automatically links the consolidated project to the original project files so that any changes made to one get reflected in the other.

HANDY TIP

You can remove the automatic link if you need to keep the files independent.

1 Create a new project 'Project2' and set the start date to 1 September.

2 Create 4 tasks of 20 days duration, link them and save the project.

	❶	Task Name	Duration	September	October	November	Dece
				23 30 06 13 20 27	04 11 18 25	01 08 15 22	29 06
1		task1	20 days				
2		task2	20 days				
3		task3	20 days				
4		task4	20 days				

3 Now create another new project called 'Consolidate' and select Insert > Project from the Menu bar.

4 Select your project and click Insert.
Your project is inserted as a summary task with an embedded project symbol in the information.

REMEMBER

Clear the Link to Project check box before inserting if you don't want them linked.

5 Now insert Project2 after your original project.

6 Expand both projects (ignoring any scheduling conflicts). The projects are set out in a consolidated view.

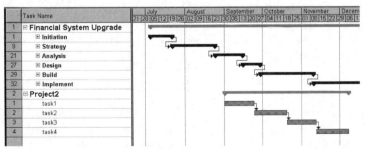

Resource Pools

If you are going to have resources working on several projects, you don't want to have to maintain the same resources in more than one place.

Microsoft Project allows you to use a resource pool so that you can coordinate the use of the shared resources.

You can either set up a new project file to hold your resource pool or you can designate an existing project as holding the resource pool.

1 Open your original project in Resource Sheet view. The resources are all listed. Don't close the project.

2 Open your new 'Project2' in Resource Sheet view. There are no resources in the project.

3 Select Tools > Resources from the Menu bar and click Share Resources.

4 Click 'Use resources', click the From down arrow and select your project from the list. Leave 'Pool takes preference' selected and click OK.

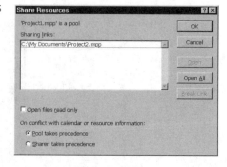

The resource list from the pool (your original project) is now displayed in the Resource Sheet for Project2.

5 Select Window > Your Project to switch back to your original project.

6 Select Tools > Resources from the Menu bar and click Share Resources. The Share Resources dialog box opens displaying the sharing links to Project2.

When you open your original project again it will ask you if you want to give write access to other projects.

Resolving Over-allocations

Once you have set up a resource pool and begin sharing resources between several projects you will need to deal with resource over-allocations. Fortunately, it is very similar to dealing with resource over-allocations in a single project.

1 Open your original project file. The Open Resource Pool dialog box opens.

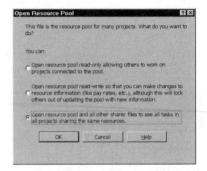

2 Select the 'Open resource pool and all other sharer files' option and click OK. The project file opens and the links are displayed.

3 Select the External tab, select task 1 (in Project2) and click Accept and Close. A pseudo task 21 (task 1 in Project 2) is inserted.

4 Select Tools > Resource Levelling from the Menu bar, select Automatic calculation and click OK. Task 22 (Analysis) has been slipped back to start on 22 September to allow pseudo task 21 (task 1 on Project2) to be completed in line with the dependency we set from task 20 (Report to Management).

Before making changes on multiple projects save all your project files!

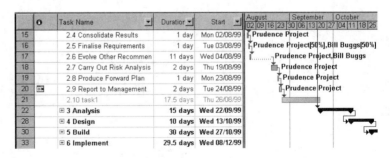

Dealing with over-allocations on multiple project is more complex than with single projects, but it can be done.

Inter-Project Dependencies

As well as consolidating projects and sharing resources you might have inter-project dependencies. This is where a task in one project is dependent on a task in another project. Dependencies between tasks in different projects can have all the usual dependency types and lag and lead time.

Microsoft Project deals with this by creating new pseudo tasks in each of the linked projects that represent the link.

1 Open the consolidated project file (ignoring any warnings) and expand task 9 (Strategy) on your original project.

You can also change the start date through the Task Information box.

2 Select task 20 (Report to Management) and drag it back so that it starts after task 19 (Produce Forward Plan). Remove the constraint when prompted.

3 Position the cursor over the middle of task 20 bar on the Gantt Chart. The cursor changes to a four headed arrow symbol.

4 Drag from task 20 on project 1 to task 2 on project 2 and release the mouse button. A link is established.

5 Click the Save button, click 'Yes to All' and close all projects.

6 Open Project2 and click OK to open the Resource Pool. Task 20 (Report to Management) from your original project is shown as pseudo task ID 1 (Report to Management) on Project2.

	ⓘ	Task Name	Duration	September 23 30 06 13 20 27	October 04 11 18 25	November 01 08 15 22
1	▦	Report to Management	2.29 days			
2		task1	20 days		Prudence Project	
3		task2	20 days			
4		task3	20 days			
5		task4	20 days			

Advanced Topics

In this chapter we take a look at Earned Value Analysis, customising the Gantt Chart and Toolbars, setting up a workgroup for the project team and using it to allocate work and request status reports.

Covers

Chapter Seventeen

Earned Value Analysis

Earned Value Analysis is a way of measuring project progress in terms of the cost of production.

Earned Value is nothing to do with the benefits of a project, just the costs.

At the planning stage the total cost of producing each product (deliverable), and therefore the project in total, is produced. This will typically consist of the resource costs plus any other fixed costs (materials, equipment, fees, etc.) which may be incurred. In earned value terms this cost is treated as the value (or worth) of the product.

As each product or deliverable is produced (or even part completed if you wish to measure work in progress), the actual cost of producing it will be known from the time and cost data that you have input for the project.

Using the budget and actual cost, the following three variables are produced:

Budgeted Cost of Work Scheduled (BCWS): This is the budgeted cost of the work planned to be done in the time being measured. This is the baselined planned expenditure.

Budgeted Cost of Work Performed (BCWP): This is the budgeted cost of the work that has actually been completed in the time being measured. It is sometimes referred to as the Earned Value as it is what it *should* have cost us to produce the work we have actually completed.

Actual Cost of Work Performed (ACWP): This is what it has actually cost us to perform the work we have actually completed.

Using the above three figures, a number of calculations can be performed to measure progress in cost terms, such as:

Schedule Variation = BCWP–BCWS (how much we should have spent to produce what we have, minus planned expenditure).

In simple terms, any calculation that gives a negative result is not good!

Cost Variation = BCWP–ACWP (how much we should have spent to produce what we have, minus what we have actually spent).

Microsoft Project has an Earned Value Report and an Earned Value Resource Table. You can also export earned value data to a spreadsheet such as Excel to produce more sophisticated charts and graphs.

1 Open your project in Gantt Chart view, display all tasks for the first two phases then select Project > Project Information from the Menu bar.
In the Project Information dialog box set the Status date to the date you have input actual data to (12/08/99).

2 Select View > Reports, Costs and Earned Value Report. The Earned Value report is produced.

Earned Value as of Wed 14/07/99
Financial System Upgrade
Your Name

ID	Task Name	BCWS	BCWP	ACWP	DV	CV
2	Agree Project Objectives	£160.00	£160.00	£160.00	£0.00	£0.00
3	Identify Stakeholders	£160.00	£160.00	£160.00	£0.00	£0.00
4	Identify Project Team	£640.00	£640.00	£640.00	£0.00	£0.00
5	Identify Business Case	£400.00	£400.00	£400.00	£0.00	£0.00
6	Analyse the Risks	£201.00	£187.00	£155.00	-£14.00	£32.00
7	Produce Outline Project Plan	£0.00	£0.00	£0.00	£0.00	£0.00
8	Project Approval	£0.00	£0.00	£0.00	£0.00	£0.00
11	Interview Managers	£0.00	£0.00	£0.00	£0.00	£0.00
12	Interview Staff	£0.00	£0.00	£0.00	£0.00	£0.00
13	Produce Draft Requirements	£0.00	£0.00	£0.00	£0.00	£0.00
14	Feedback Sessions	£0.00	£0.00	£0.00	£0.00	£0.00
15	Consolidate Results	£0.00	£0.00	£0.00	£0.00	£0.00
16	Finalise Requirements	£0.00	£0.00	£0.00	£0.00	£0.00
17	Evolve Other Recommendations	£0.00	£0.00	£0.00	£0.00	£0.00
18	Carry Out Risk Analysis	£0.00	£0.00	£0.00	£0.00	£0.00
19	Produce Forward Plan	£0.00	£0.00	£0.00	£0.00	£0.00
20	Report to Management	£0.00	£0.00	£0.00	£0.00	£0.00
21	task1	£0.00	£0.00	£0.00	£0.00	£0.00
		£1,561.00	£1,547.00	£1,515.00	-£14.00	£32.00

3 To use the Earned Value Table switch to Resource Usage view, select View > Table > More Tables > Earned Value from the Menu bar and click Apply.

4 To export Earned Value date for use in a spreadsheet select File > Save As from the Menu bar.
Click the Save as type down arrow and select 'Microsoft Excel Workbook' (or 'CSV' for other spreadsheets).
Click Save and the Export Format dialog box opens.
Select 'Earned Value Information' and click Save.
Your earned value data is saved in the required format for you to open in your spreadsheet.

Customising the Gantt Chart

There are a number of things that you can customise on the Gantt Chart (and indeed on other views as well) to make it look the way that you want. The colour and style of the various elements that appear on the schedule can be changed along with the font of any text.

1 Open your project in Gantt Chart view and expand all tasks. Notice that the summary tasks are all displayed in bold.

You can select multiple items by holding down Ctrl.

2 Select the task name field of task 1 (Initiation) and click the Bold button on the Toolbar to turn it off. The text is now displayed as normal text.
Select the other summary task names and turn bold off.

3 Select Format > Bar Styles from the Menu bar. The Bar Styles dialog box opens.

Scroll down to External Tasks (currently a grey solid bar), select it and change the pattern and colour of the middle bar to lines and turquoise.

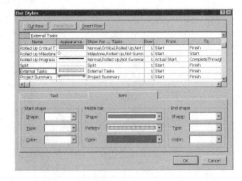

Click OK and external task 21 (task 1 from Project 2) is now displayed in the new style.

4 Select View > Toolbars > Drawing to open the Drawing Toolbar and click the Text Box button.

5 Drag to create a box to the left of task 21, type "Project 2 involvement for Project Manager" and click outside the box.

The text box is attached.

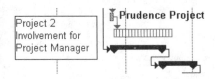

Custom Toolbars

Toolbar buttons provide quick access to frequently used Menu items. In Microsoft Project you can create your own custom Toolbars in order to put all the buttons you frequently use in one place. You can also create your own buttons for new items. Toolbars are saved in the global template so once you have created a new toolbar you can use it in any new projects.

1 Select View > Toolbars > Customise from the Menu bar. The Customise dialog box opens and lists all toolbars. It also has tabs for the Commands and display options.

2 Click New, type 'Custom Toolbar' in the name and click OK. The new toolbar is added to the list and a blank toolbar appears that looks like this. Not much to look at yet but we will add buttons to it!

3 Drag the new Toolbar away from the Customise dialog box, click the Commands tab and select View category. The View buttons and commands are displayed. Drag 'Toolbars' from Commands and drop it on your Custom Toolbar.

4 Now drag 'Reports' to the Custom Toolbar, then click Project category and add 'Project Information'. Click Close on the Customise dialog box. Your new Toolbar buttons are all active – try them!

HANDY TIP **You can add any buttons or commands to your toolbar and organise it exactly how you want it using Customise.**

5 Drag your new toolbar and drop it below the existing Toolbars. It should look like this.

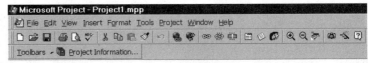

Workgroups

If you have an e-mail system or access to the Internet you can set up a workgroup in Microsoft Project which will allow you to keep in touch with your team.

For a workgroup to be set up the project manager must have Microsoft Project installed on their computer. They and the rest of the workgroup then have to have one of the following communications capabilities installed:

1.   a MAPI compliant 32 bit e-mail system

2.   a Web Browser with access to an Intranet

3.   a Web Browser with access to the Internet

For option 1 any team members that do not have Microsoft Project installed on their computer will need to have WGSETUP.EXE run on their computer to enable their e-mail to send and receive workgroup messages.

For the Intranet and Internet options a Web In Box and a Team In Box are set up to receive and track workgroup messages.

Configure a Workgroup for E-Mail

Select Tools > Options from the Menu bar, select the Workgroup tab, select e-mail in Default workgroup messaging and select Notify when new message arrives. Continue as Step 2 below.

Configure a Workgroup for Intranet/Internet

As for Step 1 above but select Web for messaging, enter the URL and message folder (for the team) and path to the Web server software and message folder (for Manager).

2   Click Set as default to apply these setting to all projects and click OK.

Allocating Assignments

Once the workgroup is set up the project manager can assign tasks and request status updates from the workgroup team members. The team members can respond and send notes.

1 Open your project and select View > Toolbars > Workgroup from the Menu bar to open the Workgroup Toolbar.

To find out what a button does, pause your cursor over it to display an explanatory message.

2 Select task 20 (Report to Management), click the Team Assign button, select 'Send message for selected task' and click OK. The Team Assign dialog box opens. Change the subject to 'Confirm Assignment' and insert 'still' in front of acceptable.

3 Click the Assign Resource button to assign a resource if one has not already been assigned and click Send. The message is sent and an additional symbol is added to the Information field for the task.

4 Pause your cursor over the Information field to display both messages.

	ⓘ	Task Name	Duration	Start
19		2.8 Produce Forward Plan	1 day	Mon 23/08/99
20	⊞ ✉	2.9 Report to Management	2 days	Tue 24/08/99
21		⊞ This task has a 'Start No Earlier Than' constraint on Mon 23/08/99.	17.5 days	Thu 26/08/99
22			15 days	Thu 26/08/99
28		✉ There has not yet been a response to all the TeamAssign messages for this task.	10 days	Fri 17/09/99
30			30 days	Fri 01/10/99
33			47 days	Fri 12/11/99

Status Reporting

As well as being able to allocate assignments to the workgroup, you can also request and submit status reports by e-mail or over the Web.

Requesting a Status Report

1   Open your project and in Project Information change the status date to 19/07/99.

2   Select task 6 (Analyse the Risks) and task 7 (Produce Outline Project Plan).

3   Click the Team Status button on the Workgroup Toolbar.
    The Team Status dialog box appears with the selected tasks and assigned resources.

4   Make any changes required to the subject, message, etc. and click Send.
    The message is sent and the Information field on both tasks is updated with a symbol.

Submitting a Status Report

1   On receipt of the Team Status Request message, enter the actual work performed for the period, the estimated work remaining for the task and any comments.

Task Name	Start	Completed	Remaining	Comments
Analyse the Risks	Thu 08/07/99	13.5h	2h	
Produce Outline Project Plan	Fri 16/07/99	0h	8h	

2   Type any required message in the Message box and click Send. Your status report is submitted.

Project Methodology

In this chapter we take a final look at some project methodologies and how they might help (or hinder) you in the effective management of your project.

Covers

Chapter Eighteen

Project Methodologies

While Microsoft Project provides an excellent project planning and scheduling tool, it will only be effective if it is used within the context of a properly managed project.

Project Management is a large subject and this book does not claim to be the last word on it! However, we have attempted to include some hints and tips on good project management practice where applicable.

This chapter is intended to give an overview of some of the methodologies that are available to assist in your project management. The methodologies included have all proven to work well with Microsoft Project.

If you work for a larger organisation (or even a smaller one that is focused on strategy) you are quite likely to have some project management standards and methodologies in place. If so, you should obviously use them together with Microsoft Project to manage your project. If not then this chapter may help.

What are Project Methodologies?

Project methodologies tend to fall into two main groups: Project Management methodologies and Systems Development methodologies. The former are applicable to all projects, whatever their objectives. The latter are only applicable to computer systems development projects. It is not possible to cover all the methodologies currently available, but this chapter covers four of the major ones in current use. What the methodologies set out to do is help you manage the function, time and cost forces acting on your project.

HANDY TIP **The forces are often stated as Quality, Time and Cost. In this context Quality and Functionality are interchangeable.**

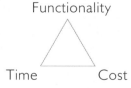

Functionality

Time   Cost

Changing any one will impact one or both of the others. For instance, if you increase the functionality of the project it will either take longer or cost more (or both).

The four methodologies and their background and use are as follows:

PRINCE 2

PRINCE has proved to be one of the most successful and popular project management methodologies. With the introduction of version 2, all reference to computer development was removed and the methodology became truly generic. It is suitable for any type of project and has been well proven in practice.

Oracle CASE*Method

The Oracle CASE*Method is again a project management methodology, but in contrast to PRINCE, Oracle's methodology assumes that the project is to develop or purchase computer software. However, despite this assumption, it can still be used with equal success on non-computer projects.

SSADM

Structured System Analysis and Design Method (SSADM) is exactly what it says. It is highly structured and focuses on the Analysis and Design stages of computer systems development projects. In fact it covers these stages in great detail. It also uses the traditional waterfall approach (sometimes referred to as the cascade method) to systems development. In this approach the requirements (functionality) are frozen early in the project and the approach is rigid. One stage cannot begin until the previous stage has been completed and signed off.

DSDM

Dynamic Systems Development Method (DSDM) represents current thinking about the most effective way to develop a business system. In this approach the requirements (functionality) are only agreed at a very strategic business level and are allowed to develop dynamically through the analysis, design and even build stages of the project. It achieves this through the use of prototypes and business models.

SSADM

The Structured Systems Analysis and Design Method (SSADM) is the UK government's standard method for carrying out the systems analysis and design stages of an information technology (IT) project. It breaks them into five modules and seven discrete stages:

Feasibility Study (FS)
Stage 0 – Feasibility (not really part of the project)

Requirements Analysis (RA)
Stage 1 – Investigation of Current Environment
Stage 2 – Business Systems Options

Requirements Specification (RS)
Stage 3 – Specification of Definition of Requirements

Logical Systems Specification (LS)
Stage 4 – Technical System Options
Stage 5 – Logical Design

Physical Design (PD)
Stage 6 – Physical Design

By taking this approach the requirements are gradually evolved and agreed and frozen by stage 3. The system is then designed (based on these frozen requirements) through the next 3 stages.

The advantages of this approach are: a) there will be less unknown factors and therefore estimates of time and cost are likely to be more accurate; b) it is possible to contract out discrete work packages to different suppliers as there are well documented requirements and procedures; and c) it is well suited to fixed, well-known requirements.

The disadvantages are: a) it is rigid and does not allow for requirements to develop through the project; and b) it tends to be long-winded and can extend the duration of a project compared to other methodologies.

It represents the fixed functionality approach, so cost and time are the variables that can be changed.

DSDM

The Dynamic Systems Development method (DSDM) is a Rapid Application Development (RAD) methodology. It is more or less the exact opposite of the SSADM approach. In DSDM the Time is fixed, the Cost (of resources) is fixed as much as possible and the Functionality (requirements) that will be met is allowed to change.

It uses five stages which map onto the traditional project stages as follows:

Feasibility Study
Not really part of the project but this is where the decision to adopt a RAD approach has to be taken. It is a pre-project activity.

Business Study
This is traditionally the Strategy Stage which identifies and baselines the high-level (strategic) business requirements.

Functional Model Iteration
This is traditionally the Analysis Stage which fleshes out the requirements. In DSDM it does it by producing iterative prototypes.

Design and Build Iteration
This is traditionally two stages: the Design Stage (which determines how the requirements will be met) and the Build Stage (which carries it out). In DSDM Build is actually the creation of the prototypes and their documentation (which takes place in both iteration stages).

Implementation
This is the same as the traditional Implementation Stage.

The advantages are: a) real business requirements are delivered in the shortest time; and b) costs are usually controlled because of the fixed time scale.

The disadvantages are: a) it will not work in rigid organisations as the decisions are made on the fly; and b) it needs fully committed users with the ability to make business decisions (but perhaps this is an advantage!).

PRINCE 2

PRINCE stands for **PR**ojects **IN** a **C**ontrolled **E**nvironment (and spell checkers always want to change that!). It does not concern itself with what the project is about, just how it is managed. It defines a project management structure and project management processes (tasks and activities) and products (deliverables) that will work with any project.

The main processes are:

Start Up the Project (SU)
Which is actually just a short pre-project activity.

Initiate the Project (IP)
The first stage of the project which formally gets it under way and plans it (Initiation Stage).

Control the Stage (CS)
This process together with the next one is carried out for each of the other stages of the project. Whether it is just one stage (Do It); the traditional Analysis, Design, Build and Implement Stages; the DSDM Stages or just periods of time.

Manage Stage Boundaries (SB)
Deals with the stage approval and start activities.

Close the Project (CP)
These are supplemented by three other processes:

Direct the Project (DP)
This defines the project board or sponsor's role.

Planning (PL)
Takes place during SU, IP and MP.

Manage Product Delivery (MP)
Defines how the actual work production is controlled.

The PRINCE 2 methodology is flexible enough to work with any of the other three methodologies covered in the chapter or indeed any other development, study or construction methodology.

Oracle CASE*Method

Computer Aided System Engineering (CASE) was a term coined to cover the automation of systems design and development. It includes both the tools (design, modelling and prototyping) and the approach (methodology). Oracle developed their CASE*Method to compliment their CASE tool products but it is completely independent of them and is a methodology in its own right.

The are two reasons for including it in this chapter. Firstly, it represents an excellent example of the traditional approach to project management. Secondly, it is a widely used methodology.

It defines the following project stages:

Strategy
The objective of the Strategy Stage is to produce a set of business models (requirements) with a plan of how they will be developed.

Analysis
The Analysis Stage determines what has to be done in order to meet the business requirements (but not yet how),

Design
The Design Stage work out how it is to be done and how the business requirements will be met.

Build
This is the traditional 'Do It' stage. The new system, whatever it is, will be constructed or built.

User Documentation
Traditionally this is part of the Build Stage but this methodology treats it as a separate but parallel stage.

Transition
This is the traditional Implementation Stage.

The method also specifies in detail the tasks, activities and deliverables. These largely concentrate on the technical rather than the management side of project management.

The Final Word

Putting it all together, Microsoft Project is an excellent project planning, scheduling and monitoring tool. By adding the appropriate project management processes or methodologies you really can stay in control of your project.

PRINCE 2 gives an excellent framework for management and a quality focus for a project. It (or sometimes a subset of it) is becoming mandatory in an increasing number of organisations. It defines a project start up and initiation stage better than any of the other methodologies.

SSADM is a mandatory requirement in some government (and quasi-government) organisations. If so, you will need to use it. If not, it is probably best avoided.

Oracle CASE*Method may well be in use in organisations that use the Oracle DBMS (DataBase Management System) although the two are completely freestanding. It also offers a useful pre-defined list of tasks, activities and deliverables for all the major project stages (except Initiation).

DSDM is a relatively new methodology although it is based on well proven principles (e.g. Peter Coad's object oriented analysis and design books). It is an excellent approach to the rapid development of computer systems that really will meet business needs.

So there you go. If you have a free choice or are involved in a non-IT project, have a look at PRINCE. If you are running a systems development project PRINCE + DSDM provides an excellent blend of formal management and a flexible approach. For package selection PRINCE + CASE*Method should cover everything you need. Finally if you have to use SSADM it does at least work with PRINCE!

And finally, never forget:

Murphy's 4th Law

The light at the end of the tunnel will probably turn out to be the headlamp of an oncoming train!

Index

U

V

W

Z